You Become What You Think

Harnessing the Power of Positive Thinking

Phoenix Emerald

Please consult a licensed professional before attempting any techniques outlined in this book.

By reading this document, the reader agrees that under no circumstances is the author responsible for any losses, direct or indirect, that are incurred as a result of the use of the information contained within this document, including, but not limited to, errors, omissions, or inaccuracies.

Table of Contents

INTRODUCTION 1

CHAPTER 1: THE POWER OF POSITIVE THINKING...................5

DEFINING POSITIVE THINKING..6
   Differentiation From Optimism.....................................7
   Cognitive Aspect 8
   Realism in Positive Thinking..8
HISTORICAL PERSPECTIVES ON POSITIVE THINKING.............9
   Ancient Philosophies...10
   Renaissance and Enlightenment Thinkers 11
   The 20th Century Movements 11
NEUROLOGICAL BASIS OF POSITIVITY...................................12
   Brain Plasticity and Positive Thinking 13
   Neurochemical Effects 13
   Impact on the Stress Response 14
POSITIVE PSYCHOLOGY PIONEERS 14
   Martin Seligman 15
   Mihaly Csikszentmihalyi...15
   Barbara Fredrickson...16

CHAPTER 2: THE PSYCHOLOGY BEHIND YOUR THOUGHTS....19

COGNITIVE PROCESSES AND THOUGHT PATTERNS.............20
   Neural Pathways and Habitual Thinking 21
   Role of the Prefrontal Cortex 22
   Cognitive Dissonance...22
INFLUENCE OF EMOTIONS ON THINKING 24
   Emotional Reasoning...25
   Mood-Congruent Memory..26
   Impact of Anxiety and Stress on Cognitive Functions 27

ROLE OF PERCEPTION IN THOUGHT FORMATION 27
  Selective Perception...*28*
  Perceptual Set Theory..*29*
  The Influence of Social Norms *29*
IMPACT OF MEMORY ON THOUGHTS 30
  Flashbulb Memories *31*
  Schemas and Stereotypes......................................*31*
  The Role of the Hippocampus in Memory and Thought..*31*

CHAPTER 3: TRANSFORMING NEGATIVE THOUGHTS 33

IDENTIFYING NEGATIVE THOUGHT PATTERNS..................................34
  Common Cognitive Distortions *35*
  Triggers and Context *38*
  Self-Monitoring Techniques...................................*39*
UNDERSTANDING THE SOURCES OF NEGATIVE THOUGHTS.................46
  Influence of Childhood Experiences *46*
  Cultural and Societal Conditioning *47*
  Stress and Lifestyle Factors.................................*47*
THE ROLE OF SELF-AWARENESS IN THOUGHT TRANSFORMATION 48
  Mindfulness Practices..*49*
  Feedback from Others *52*
  Emotional Intelligence Development...........................*52*
REFRAMING TECHNIQUES 52
  Cognitive Restructuring *53*
  Perspective Shifting *54*
  Use of Positive Affirmations *54*

CHAPTER 4: THE IMPACT OF CULTURE AND ENVIRONMENT.57

ENVIRONMENTAL INFLUENCES ON MINDSET...................................57
  Urban vs. Rural Mindsets.....................................*58*
  Green Spaces and Mental Health *59*
  Design and Architecture's Role...............................*60*
THE ROLE OF FAMILY IN SHAPING THOUGHTS 61

Modeling Positive Thinking..*62*

Communication Styles *62*

Handling Family Conflict....................................*63*

MEDIA IMPACT ON THOUGHT PROCESSES *64*

Filtering Media Consumption *65*

Balancing Awareness and Overwhelm *65*

Social Media as a Tool for Positive Connection *66*

SOCIOECONOMIC FACTORS AND THEIR IMPACT ON THOUGHT PATTERNS

....*67*

Economic Stress and Mental Health *67*

The Role of Community Support *68*

Social Mobility and Positivity..*68*

CHAPTER 5: BUILDING POSITIVE HABITS **71**

THE PSYCHOLOGY OF HABIT FORMATION *71*

Neurological Underpinnings *72*

Reward Systems in Habit Formation.................................*73*

Role of Trigger Identification *74*

SETTING UP FOR SUCCESS *74*

Optimal Environment Design..*75*

Routine Structuring for Positive Thinking *75*

Tools and Resources *76*

SMALL HABITS, BIG IMPACT *76*

Incremental Approach *77*

The Power of Mini Habits *77*

Celebrating Small Wins...*78*

THE ROLE OF CONSISTENCY *78*

Overcoming Resistance...*78*

Building Resilience Through Routine..........................*79*

Accountability Mechanisms..*79*

CHAPTER 6: MASTERING RESILIENCE AND THRIVING IN ADVERSITY **81**

THE COMPONENTS OF RESILIENCE 82

    Flexibility and Mental Agility *82*

    Perseverance Through Positivity *83*

    Positive Thinking as a Resilience Builder *84*

PSYCHOLOGICAL TRAITS FOR THRIVING 85

    Courage to Face Uncertainty *86*

    Adaptability in Changing Circumstances *86*

    Impact of Emotional Resilience *88*

LEARNING FROM SETBACKS 89

    Reframing Setbacks *89*

    Positive Feedback Loops *91*

    Setbacks as Windows of Opportunity *92*

PREPARE FOR A POSITIVE OUTCOME: ADOPTING A GROWTH MINDSET IN ADVERSE CONDITIONS 93

    When Challenges Become Opportunities *93*

    Continual Learning and Adaptation *94*

    Resilience Through Learning *95*

CHAPTER 7: THE ROLE OF POSITIVITY IN RELATIONSHIPS 97

FOUNDATIONS OF POSITIVE INTERACTIONS 98

    Principles of Positive Communication *98*

    Role of Positive Language *100*

    Feedback Loops in Communication *102*

COMMUNICATION SKILLS FOR POSITIVE ENGAGEMENT 102

    Active Listening Techniques *103*

    Effective Use of Affirmations *105*

    Constructive Feedback *106*

BUILDING EMOTIONAL INTELLIGENCE 107

    Self-Regulation and Emotional Responsiveness *108*

    Empathy Development Practices *108*

    Emotional Awareness in Communication *109*

IMPACT OF POSITIVITY ON CONFLICT RESOLUTION 110

    Transforming Conflicts with Positivity *111*

Preventative Positivity: The Role of Optimism in Resolving Disputes *113*

CHAPTER 8: VISUALIZATION AND GOAL SETTING 115

BASICS OF VISUALIZATION 115
Neurological Basis of Visualization *116*
Psychological Impact *116*
Visualization as a Habit *117*
TYPES OF VISUALIZATION TECHNIQUES 117
Guided Imagery for Specific Goals *118*
Vision Boards to Sustain Motivation *119*
Mental Rehearsals for Skill Enhancement *121*
INCORPORATING VISUALIZATION INTO DAILY ROUTINES 121
Morning Visualization Routines *122*
Visualization Breaks During the Day *124*
Evening Reflection Through Visualization *124*
ROLE OF VISUALIZATION IN PROBLEM-SOLVING 125
Visualizing Outcomes to Enhance Decision-Making *125*
Creative Problem Solving with Visualization *126*
Strategic Visualization in Professional Settings *126*

CHAPTER 9: MAINTAINING YOUR MENTAL HEALTH 129

IDENTIFYING STRESSORS AND TRIGGERS 130
Personal Reflection and Journaling *131*
Mindfulness and Awareness Training *133*
Environmental Adjustments *134*
ROLE OF PHYSICAL ACTIVITY IN MENTAL HEALTH 135
Exercise as a Natural Antidepressant *135*
Routine Integration *136*
Social Sports and Group Fitness *137*
NUTRITION AND MENTAL WELL-BEING 137
Brain Foods for Positive Thinking *138*
Impact of Hydration on Cognitive Function *142*

Meal Planning for Mental Health *143*

Sleep's Impact on Mental Health 147

Sleep Hygiene Practices *148*

Link Between Sleep and Emotional Regulation *149*

Technological Impacts on Sleep *149*

CHAPTER 10: LIVING A POSITIVELY TRANSFORMED LIFE 151

Sustaining Positivity in Daily Life 152

Routine Positive Affirmations *152*

Positive Interaction Rituals *154*

Mindset Resets *155*

Reflective Practices for Self-Assessment 155

Structured Journaling Techniques *156*

Meditative Reflection *158*

Feedback Loops with Trusted Peers *159*

Balancing Positivity with Realistic Expectations 159

Setting Achievable Goals *160*

Embracing Constructive Criticism *162*

Awareness of Cognitive Biases *163*

Adapting Positivity to Changing Life Stages 163

Age-Specific Positive Thinking Techniques *164*

Anticipating Life Transitions *165*

Lifelong Learning as a Tool for Adaptation *166*

CONCLUSION **169**

REFERENCES **171**

Introduction

Positive thinkers don't ignore the negatives; they see the whole picture. Being a positive thinker is not about forcing a positive outlook on things. Instead, it's about adopting a constructive mindset that allows you to progress in good and bad times. When you think positively, seeing a problem becomes less about the issue and more about what you can do to remedy it or how you can learn from it. Positive thinking is all about actively seeking out and focusing on what you can do to perform and be productive in every area of your life. A positive thinker sees a challenge for what it is, and instead of denying it, they take out their toolbox of positive strategies and find solutions for what they can manage. Positive thinkers also know to let go of what they can't control so they can optimize their energy by focusing on and fixing what they can control.

How often has thinking negatively about a situation gotten you in a rut? Perhaps, you've overthought your friend's actions or misjudged their demeanor during a conversation, making it hard to communicate constructively. Maybe you've received negative feedback from your colleagues and bosses, leaving you unable to apply the advice in future projects. Too often, negativity takes hold of your life in ways you may or might not have realized. However, adopting a positive mindset is here to change all of that. Positive thinking reshapes your life toward solutions, connection, and growth. You can say goodbye to misunderstandings, self-pity slumps, and feeling stuck—and hello to self-confidence and development. Positive thinking is rooted in breaking negative cycles so you can improve and build upon your experiences.

Sometimes you, like many of us, can set mental roadblocks in the form of negative thinking that keeps you from achieving what you seek to achieve. Yet, positive thinking is a power that you can harness to change those patterns and develop yourself. You can enhance your quality of life by changing your mindset and fostering self-improvement. A positive mindset can transform relationships, improve communication, cultivate empathy, and strengthen interpersonal connections. You'll start to approach conversations, feedback, and relationships from a mindset that nourishes and appreciates what you have. For example, rather than seeing your boss's feedback as an attack, positive thinking will help you see it as guidance for future improvement. Becoming a positive thinker is a way to overcome personal and professional challenges, making achieving greater life success and satisfaction possible.

You become what you think. Your thoughts about yourself and the world around you are crucial because they influence your actions and decisions. Your thoughts affect how you set and achieve goals. Thinking patterns also contribute to the trajectory you take in life. Your way of thinking either helps you stay motivated and get through adversity or leads to giving up. Embracing positive thinking positions you to experience a positive life. Positive thinking enhances resilience and gives you the grit to manage tough times. It also offers a new perspective to view setbacks as growth opportunities. If you are ready to change your thinking so you can transform your life, look no further.

Positive thinking is not just a concept but a practical tool that can be systematically applied through specific strategies and exercises to improve daily life. The growth you seek in life is a reflection of your dedication and determination to see your life transformed in a way that harnesses the power of positive thinking. It is vital to understand that your thoughts significantly influence how you feel and behave. So, changing your thought patterns profoundly impacts your life. Positive thinking has tangible benefits for both mental and physical health, including reduced stress, improved immune function, and overall better health outcomes.

This book offers advice with scientific support about the importance of a positive mindset to help you understand its benefits. You will begin to notice how imperative your mindset is to your development, health, and fulfillment. The goal is to provide you with techniques and mechanisms to use as a foundation for positive thinking. As you continue reading, you'll be equipped with concrete, actionable strategies to maintain a positive mindset.

Eventually, you'll be able to handle stress constructively by using affirmations and visualization. This book explores core concepts and themes such as the science of positivity, strategies for transforming negative thoughts, building resilience, goal setting, and the role of positivity in relationships. Written to help you thrive at work and in your home life, it offers numerous insights into positive thinking.

Implementing the tools from this book into your daily life will enrich your experiences and inspire you to approach situations confidently. You'll be able to think in ways that foster personal and professional development. Through a series of motivational stories, case studies, and evidence of success, by the end of the book you should feel encouraged to embrace positive thinking and allow it to transform your life.

Chapter 1:
The Power of Positive Thinking

Imagine five great things happening for you, accompanied by two not-so-great things. Are you more likely to fixate on the five great things or the two not-so-great things? Many of us are likely to spend the day beating ourselves up for the two no-so-great things. This realization relates directly to the concept of positive thinking. Reflecting positively on our lives is about embracing the five good things that happen while improving or working through the other two. Positive thinking acknowledges that the two not-so-great things might suck, but it's not the end of the world. Being a positive thinker involves allowing your mind to explore endless possibilities in favor of your personal growth. It's not about beating yourself up for what didn't work out or pretending the good experiences are all there is—it's a happy medium.

Positive thinking contributes to individual health by reducing stress and increasing feelings of competence. It gives one a more meaningful outlook on life and its experiences. Learn more about positive thinking to make it a valuable part of your approach to situations. When learning something new, it's always beneficial to start with the basics. As such, this chapter explores what positive thinking is by differentiating it from optimism while unpacking the history of positivity and its pioneers.

Defining Positive Thinking

Positive thinking isn't about making light of your problems but finding ways to cope with challenges and address adversity head-on. When you think positively, you lead with a hopeful attitude, believing that things will go well with every step you take to overcome hardships. A positive mindset chooses to take the good things into account when making decisions. Doing so helps you sort through inconveniences by noticing the value in your experiences.

For example, you leave the house early, rushing for a meeting, only to be stuck in traffic caused by an unpredictable road accident. Instead of getting annoyed or feeling frustrated, positive thinking allows you to accept the situation for what it is—random and unpredictable—while realizing that you can make the most of it. For many, being stuck in traffic is angering, but for positive thinkers, it's an opportunity for quiet time before work, enjoying their on-the-go breakfast, or creating a mental checklist of things to do during the day.

Positive thinking offers you the bright side in seemingly dark times. When you think positively, you allow your mind to shift from distress to a state of acceptance and productivity. You start to think more rationally about situations and let go of the obsession with the situation being different. Though optimism and positivity tend to be used interchangeably, there are subtle differences. Exploring these differences can help you define positive thinking a bit more so you can apply it to personal experiences.

Differentiation From Optimism

Optimism assumes something good will happen (Shero, 2019). It hopes that, in the end, things will work themselves out. Unlike optimism, positive thinking goes a step further. Positive thinking considers what response you will have, regardless of the situation. Although you may hope things work out, positive thinking doesn't necessarily make assumptions about outcomes. Instead, it prepares you to manage whatever situation confronts you productively.

Positive thinking is more than expecting the best outcome in situations; it involves actively reframing your challenges. A positive mindset changes how you see challenges to focus on opportunities, lessons, and solutions. Rather than just hoping for change, positive thinking is about taking constructive steps toward implementing the changes you want to see.

Optimism, on the other hand, is more about the attitude aspect of positivity. Optimistic people are filled with hope for good outcomes but don't always act on their hopeful attitude, which leads to blind positivity. You can even think of optimism as the starting point of positive thinking because you need hope to motivate you to act. All in all, positivity and optimism are collaborative.

When used correctly, both can help you accomplish what you set out to achieve.

Cognitive Aspect

Every action begins in the mind. When you think and believe in a thought, you are likely to act on that belief. That's why reframing your thinking to become more positive leads to beneficial actions. The cognitive aspect of positive thinking involves recognizing your thinking patterns, deliberately finding solutions, and focusing on potentially positive outcomes. Harnessing positive thinking ensures that you create a productive cognitive environment to get your mind to push you toward acting productively.

Realism in Positive Thinking

Believing that positive thinking is equivalent to ignoring reality or denying the negatives is a common misconception. Realism in positive thinking involves confronting issues with solutions, hope, and proactivity. It's about recognizing that your positivity must be rooted in actionable steps or ideas that can lead to noticeable changes.

Also, realism in positive thinking recognizes that setbacks are a part of life's journey. It's okay to hope that things go your way and put in the work to get a good outcome, but realism in positivity involves embracing the alternative if things don't work out how you hope. For example, you prepare for a meeting about a possible promotion. You have all your points ready, and you leave the room feeling like you got the promotion. Suddenly, a call from your boss states that your presentation was excellent, and they see the potential in you for future promotions, but this particular opportunity is right for someone else.

Realism in positive thinking allows you to acknowledge that your contribution was impressive and that things didn't work out simply because it's just not your time yet. You can still hold on to the belief that when the time is right, the promotion will be yours. The rejection translates as redirection, and you know you'll put just as much effort into the next presentation should the offer arise. Realism in positive thinking recognizes that every experience, good or unpleasant, is imperative for your development. So you can take the good with the bad when it comes.

Historical Perspectives on Positive Thinking

Harnessing the power of positive thinking isn't as new as you might think. Western culture has had a rapid rise in philosophies on positivity, pushing the message of how thoughts shape reality and how people can tap into their minds to find love and create success in their lives (Roginski, n.d.). As far back as the first century, Epictetus has a record stating, "The thing that upsets people is not so much what happens, but what they think about what happens" (*The Origins of Positive Thinking*, 2018). Great historical authors and writers addressed the human condition and its link to one's mindset. The perspective of positive thinking hinges on the understanding that how we think and perceive things genuinely creates what we experience.

Historical perspectives on positive thinking rose to prominence in the early and mid-20th century. As time passed, thinkers, philosophers, and businessmen started sharing this new thought movement. The power of positivist thinking expanded from positive psychology to a secular perspective. The positive thinking perspective continued through pioneers such as Ralph Waldo Emerson and Martin Seligman. They've even left a fingerprint on the approach we see in motivational speakers, positivity posts, and mindset podcasts today.

Ancient Philosophies

Historically, positive thinking is rooted in multiple religions' ideals and evolved through the world's New Thought Movement (*The History of the Power of Positive Thinking*, n.d.). Ancient philosophies, including Stoicism and Buddhism, emphasize positive thinking by advocating for inner peace and control over one's reactions to external circumstances. The Stoic philosophy is driven by physics, logic, and ethics (*Stoicism*, 2023). It emphasizes the interlocking contributions of each aspect in maintaining a balanced life. Positive thinking infuses aspects of Stoicism to keep people grounded in reality as they navigate life's challenges.

On the other hand, Buddhism conveys the principle of happiness as a deep inner state of contentment (*Buddha,* n.d.). Essentially, Buddhists believe that people's reality manifests based on the quality of their thinking: "You are what you think." Buddhist teachings understand that fulfillment is found in accepting reality and mindfulness. What ancient philosophies have in common is the realization that no material possessions, external dynamics, and so on have as much power to influence the state of your physical life as your mind does.

Renaissance and Enlightenment Thinkers

The merge of the Renaissance (a period marked by learning and wisdom) and the Enlightenment (a period of awakening to knowledge concerning philosophical ideas) supported a bright worldview. The Renaissance and Enlightenment era focused on human potential and self-awareness, contributing to early positive thinking. Individualism was valued by Renaissance and Enlightenment thinkers (Lijewski, n.d.). As such, creative people began to gain popularity as artists. Philosophers saw the value in creativity and moral actions as catalysts for internal joy and happiness.

The 20th Century Movements

The rise of self-help movements in the 20th century, particularly after World War II, popularized positive thinking through figures like Norman Vincent Peale and the broader cultural embrace of psychoanalysis and personal transformation. Also, the professor of neurology and psychiatry, Viktor Frankl, founded logotherapy—an influential concept based on the power of positive thinking—in the 1930s (Madeson, 2020). Frankl believed people derive meaning and thrive from finding purpose in life.

Based on his experiences in Nazi concentration camps, Frankl found that by deriving meaning and finding purpose in situations, people were able to cope with harsh conditions (WebMD Editorial Contributors, n.d.). In other words, positive thinking, which is the process of seeking meaning and finding purpose in personal experiences, makes it possible to overcome or manage suffering. As such, logotherapy suggests that people who derive meaning or think positively tend to live healthier, more mindful, and longer lives.

Neurological Basis of Positivity

Our thoughts affect our brains. Neuroplasticity is a term used to highlight the continuous development that the brain experiences, so every thought and belief we entertain influences neurotransmitters, causing us to behave or respond a certain way (Whitaker, n.d.). Positive thinking, then, is directly linked to immune and mental health. let's take a deep dive into how.

Brain Plasticity and Positive Thinking

Positive thinking creates a feedback loop, helping your brain rewire itself in a process called neuroplasticity (Whitaker, n.d.). This means your thoughts physically change the brain's structure, enhancing areas that regulate emotions and cognitive processing. So, if you think, *Today will be a good day,* the neural pathways in your mind send that message throughout your body. It leaves you feeling at ease with the expectation of a lovely day ahead. Equally, if your day isn't going as planned, telling yourself *I can overcome this and learn from it* offers you a more enlightening experience.

Brains constantly receive and fire signals from your memories, thoughts, or external situations. When you label something as "good" or "bad," your mind works your entire body to respond accordingly. That's why triggers can often result in people lashing out even though there's no imminent danger to them. Also, that's why good times can make people behave in a way that conveys excitement and happiness. Your thoughts are constantly channeled into your responses, influencing the quality of your life. So, it must be said that positive thinking produces a chain reaction.

Neurochemical Effects

Positive thoughts increase neurotransmitters like serotonin and dopamine, which are associated with feelings of well-being and reduced stress. You get to experience feelings like gratitude, joy, and others linked to pleasure. So, thinking positively is good for brain health. When you focus on positive thoughts, you actively stimulate a positive reaction in your brain, making you happier and healthier. But the benefits of positive thinking don't stop there!

Impact on the Stress Response

Positive thinking helps modulate the brain's response to stress, potentially lowering the production of stress hormones like cortisol and reducing the overall impact of stress on the body. Stress affects all parts of the body, putting your respiratory, cardiovascular, and nervous systems at risk (*Stress Effects on The Body,* 2023). This is why reducing stress levels through positive thinking is important. Through positivity, you are better suited to manage stress, which strengthens the immune system, reduces inflammation, and lowers the risk of other illnesses as well. Positivity is your best weapon against adversity and stress. For that reason, positive thinking has become a significant component in psychology.

Positive Psychology Pioneers

Unlike mainstream psychology, which focuses on illness and cures, positive psychology focuses on preventing disease by helping people foster healthier habits and life patterns—mainly through positive thinking. The pioneers of positive psychology aimed to move away from the consideration, "What makes a person ill?" and adopt a new perspective by considering, "What makes a person healthy and happy?"

Martin Seligman

The founding father of positive psychology, Martin Seligman, defines the field as focusing on what makes life more pleasant, engaging, and fulfilling for people (Ackerman, 2018). Seligman is known for his significant role as the founder of positive psychology, his theories on learned optimism, and his emphasis on character strengths and virtues as a path to a fulfilling life. Although Martin Seligman's work provided the blueprint for positive psychology, his findings were further supported by other pioneers in the field.

Mihaly Csikszentmihalyi

Mihaly Csikszentmihalyi is noted as a cofounder of positive psychology (Oppland, 2016). Csikszentmihalyi's concept of "flow," a state of deep enjoyment and engagement in activities, hugely contributed to the direction of the field. This concept has influenced the understanding of positive experiences and their impact on life satisfaction. According to Csikszentmihalyi, "flow" refers to those moments of mind wandering when you are completely focused on challenging but accomplishable tasks. In his contribution, Csikszentmihalyi believed that life's best experiences happen when the body or mind are pulled to their limits in a voluntary determination to achieve something difficult and worthwhile.

The concept of flow is fascinating in positive psychology. It highlights that performance, goal orientation, creativity, and focus on a worthwhile task can offer a sense of fulfillment or positivity. This realization makes being in a flow state meaningful in people's lives. Examples of a flow state include working on a challenging but fun work project, solving a complex equation, or even figuring out your work-from-home schedule. The flow zone is known to help you tap into the greater purpose in life.

Men weren't the only contributors and pioneers of this great field of thought; women were valuable, too.

Barbara Fredrickson

One such woman pioneer is Barbara Fredrickson, a psychologist who focused on how action reduced negative emotions (Celestine, 2016). Fredrickson suggested a "broaden-and-build" theory, arguing that positive emotions broaden an individual's momentary thought-action repertoire, which in turn helps to build their enduring personal resources. This can range from physical and intellectual to social and psychological resources. Thought-action repertoire refers to a range of actions or perceptions thereof that's available to someone at any given time.

The idea is that a narrow thought-action repertoire causes someone's world to feel smaller, increasing the likelihood of feelings of depression, limited opportunities, and helplessness. Yet, broadening this repertoire pushes past mental limitations of what is possible. It introduces people to a whole new world of options, resulting in happier, more socially proactive people. To put it simply, the more opportunities your brain believes are out there—broad repertoire—the better you deal with things like rejection, adversity, and challenges. Therefore, the happier or more positive thinker you become. Fredrickson understood the need to broaden individual repertoire to enhance experiences, improve mental health, and build relationships.

Segiman, Csikszentmihalyi, and Fredrickson pioneered positive psychology by focusing on health, engagement, and opportunities as pillars for a satisfying life. Without these pioneers, the evidence for positive thinking and its beneficial impact on individual lives wouldn't be what it is today.

The importance of a positive mindset grew from a historical point of view to influence many areas of life in the 21st century. We see positivity in advertising, corporate speeches, health, sports, parenting, education, psychology, and many more areas of our lives. It's a perspective that shapes many religious beliefs and ways of life as well. You can take up positive thinking for yourself and see the magnificent changes that are happening in your life. The next chapter focuses on the psychology behind your thought patterns so you can address them and harness the power of positive thinking.

Chapter 2:
The Psychology Behind Your Thoughts

A thought refers to an idea formulated in the mind, associating with or representing something (Lewis, 2023). Your emotions, reactions, and experiences are all weaved together by a series of associations that you make in your mind. In other words, your encounters are shaped by how you think. Every experience you have is processed through the lens of perception.

For something to be good or bad, you must first formulate an idea of it in your mind, tying it to an association. For example, you might think of presentations as the worst thing because you associate standing in front of large audiences with that one time you embarrassed yourself at a talent show in high school. In this analogy, presentations aren't good or bad; they just *are*. However, your mental association or representation of standing in front of a crowd influences how you feel about the act of presenting.

Take the same example and imagine you have a friend who enjoys presentations. Perhaps she associates them with sharing her ideas among groups of people, allowing her to network and discover new ideas. Because she associates presenting with opportunity, your friend can view this experience as exciting. Say you ask your friend why she enjoys presenting so much; you might find she has always had a positive perception of interacting with large audiences. Her positive view of audiences could be linked to how she was the captain of the debate team or the winner of many talent shows at school.

Alternatively, it could be that she was also embarrassed in front of a crowd at some point but chose to view that moment as a learning curve rather than internalize it as humiliation. Therefore, your friend's association doesn't bring up feelings of fear when she thinks about presentations; instead, she finds herself eager to learn.

The difference between your association of audiences and hers is the lens of perception. In other words, it's the psychology behind your thoughts or ideas formulated in your mind about something that guides what happens next. This chapter delves into the cognitive mechanisms that shape people's thoughts. It explains the influence of thoughts and teaches how awareness can pave the way for mental transformation.

Cognitive Processes and Thought Patterns

Your thoughts shape perception and how you show up in the world. Sometimes, you don't even have to experience something to think a certain way about it. Consider the example above about presentations. You might tell your sibling about the fear you have of presenting. All the details of it and how you freeze every time you stand in front of a crowd. After hearing about your fear for a while, your sibling might subconsciously start to build a fear of their own about presenting in front of audiences. They might never have done it before, but hearing how sacred it makes you might have them associating the mere idea of presentations with that fear. It's amazing how the mind works!

The connection between thoughts and behaviors is rooted in cognitive processes and principles of psychology. Cognitive processes and thought patterns have the ability to impact how we think about a situation, even before it plays out. This can drastically influence our mood, responses, and perspectives at any given time.

Neural Pathways and Habitual Thinking

Neural pathways are the system of circuits constantly firing in your brain (Andruşca, 2023). These are responsible for how you respond to life's experiences. Neural pathways connect to your brain and spinal cord as ascending and descending tracts, which carry sensory and mother signals to your body. Because of this connection, you can feel somatic sensations together with conscious and reflective behaviors.

Your thoughts shape and strengthen your pathways to influence habitual processes. Repetitive thinking patterns reinforce neural pathways, making some thoughts automatic, like driving a car or reacting emotionally to specific triggers. Focusing on positive thoughts and making that a habitual cognitive process strengthens the neural pathways responsible for your joy. Equally, focusing on helplessness strengthens neural stress pathways. So, help yourself and focus on the good!

Role of the Prefrontal Cortex

When you think positively, a region of your brain known as the prefrontal cortex is stimulated toward further development. This region is responsible for managing higher-order cognitive processes, including planning, decision-making, and moderating social behavior, and it is crucial for intentional thought control (Whitaker, n.d.).

Think of the prefrontal cortex as your body's central management center. That's where all the switches and regulatory signals take place. The prefrontal cortex allows you to reflect, focus on, and control your emotions. Thinking positively stimulates the prefrontal cortex to enhance your thinking skills and sense of self-control. A happy brain means you become a more productive, influential person.

Cognitive Dissonance

Cognitive dissonance refers to situations in which conflicting beliefs lead to discomfort (Lawler, 2022). People typically strive to achieve consistency in their beliefs, attitudes, and behaviors, which influences their thought processes. However, when beliefs and behaviors misalign, cognitive dissonance occurs.

The mind sorts through experiences quite fast, so sometimes you might not notice when cognitive dissonance happens. For example, if you drop your water bottle while rushing out the door, you might first feel panic at the extra time you need to spend picking it up as it rolls across the room. At this moment, the belief is that, *I should be in the car on my way to work already*, but the frustration comes by realizing that *I still need to put my things in the car and return to the house to pick my bottle off the floor.* Instantly, the belief misaligns with the experience, causing cognitive dissonance.

However, the dissonance is reduced the moment you notice the frustration and rationalize the experience through a positive lens. So, now you can think, *I should be in the car on my way to work already, but I get to double-check if I have everything and pick up my bottle before heading out.* Instead of seeing the interruption as somewhat of a nuisance to your day, you can incorporate positive thinking to change your perspective.

On the flip side, you can use cognitive dissonance to introduce new, positive habits. For example, if you don't enjoy exercising, you can convince yourself of the benefits of a good workout. Your belief is that you don't want to exercise, but cognitive dissonance helps you exercise despite that belief. See how it works both ways?

In moments when uncomfortable misalignment occurs, as in the first example, it helps to notice the cause of your frustration. Once you become aware that cognitive dissonance is happening, you can just as quickly deploy a positive thought to reframe your perspective of the experience. Therefore, reduce the discomfort and adjust your attitude toward the situation.

Influence of Emotions on Thinking

Emotions are states of mind that evoke pleasure or displeasure in response to stimuli (Cooks-Campbell, 2022). Joy occurs when someone feels good, while anger can occur when someone feels frustrated or disappointed. It's also possible to experience mixed emotions where you experience multiple psychological states at once. For example, you can feel excited about graduation and sad that a loved one won't experience the moment with you.

Neuroscientific evidence has proven that emotions influence thinking and problem-solving skills (Cooks-Campbell, 2023). This means that your emotional state of mind affects the quality of your decisions, learning, moods, and experiences. So, regulating your emotions can help you be more clear-headed. Mental clarity enables you to make good decisions, improve focus, and curate positive experiences.

There are typically eight standard emotions that can be experienced universally. These emotions include sadness, anger, fear, joy, disgust, excitement, astonishment, and trust. No emotion is good or bad; each is simply a message of how you feel in a moment.

Understanding the importance of embracing your emotions will help you regulate them and cope better.

Emotional Reasoning

When your emotions aren't regulated, they can cause you to think unreasonably. Unmonitored emotions can cloud your judgment, leading to decision-making based heavily on your feelings rather than objective facts, often called "emotional reasoning." When your judgment is clouded, you can so easily think what you *feel* reflects reality. Yet, your emotions are very temporary and sometimes have no real (factual) basis at all. Emotional reasoning can often land you in awkward situations, creating more negative experiences for yourself.

For example, you might *feel* jealous in your relationship and use this subjective emotion as fact. Emotional reasoning in this situation would cause you to be suspicious of your partner, which can manifest as accusations and mistrust. Yet, just because you feel jealous doesn't mean there's any evidence to support your suspicion of your partner. Another example of emotional reasoning is feeling you did poorly in a test, even though the results haven't come out yet.

Emotional reasoning isn't just about basing your judgments on negative feelings; it can also happen in instances of positive thoughts. For example, you might think you should go gambling because you feel lucky, but you end up taking an unnecessary risk that costs you considerable amounts.

People who reason with their emotions often conclude what they feel is factual, sometimes without supporting evidence, and emotions make interpretations credible. Fortunately, positive thinking can help you keep your emotions in check by drawing you back to reality. With positive thinking, you either consider the validity of emotional thinking to disprove your reasoning or replace your reasoning with a more rational thought.

Mood-Congruent Memory

Mood-congruent memory is based on the understanding that a person's current mood can influence the recall of memories consistent with that mood, thereby influencing current thoughts and decisions (BetterHelp Editorial Team, 2024). The idea is that your emotions affect how you encode memories, which influences your perspective.

Mood congruency happens when you remember past experiences and those memories along with your current emotional state. So, when you experience happy emotions, you might focus on good memories. Equally, when you experience unhappy emotions, you tend to recall unpleasant memories.

Due to mood-congruent memory, the emotions you linger on can affect your experiences. So, focusing on positive thoughts is essential so you can have your good memories linger a bit longer. Positive thinking floods you with positive memories, preventing a downward spiral of emotions.

Impact of Anxiety and Stress on Cognitive Functions

A downward spiral of emotions leads to a negative ripple effect. High levels of anxiety and stress can be a part of this spiral, impairing cognitive functioning (Des Marais, 2022). It can also reduce the capacity for complex problem-solving and creative thought. In a stressful situation, your brain automatically allocates resources to help you manage stress. This means it takes energy and effort away from your cognitive functions.

Signs that anxiety and stress might be impacting your thinking can be emotional, cognitive, and physical. Some examples of the impact anxiety has on cognition include forgetfulness, rigid thinking, difficulty with focus, constant concern, and poor decision-making. To prevent either of these cognitive experiences, it's imperative to focus on positive thinking. Remember, positive thoughts can ease anxiety and stress.

Role of Perception in Thought Formation

Perception refers to how we view and experience the world. It is a sensory experience that allows us to become aware of the objects, connections, and other aspects of our respective environments. You can use your touch, sight, sound, smell, and taste to build perception. This process also makes it possible for you to detect your body's movement and position in an experience called proprioception.

People use perception to process cognitive information. For example, you might smell food that makes you remember Thanksgiving dinner with family. Your perception is linked to the formation and utilization of memory. It enables you to identify and respond to stimuli in various situations.

Selective Perception

When people subconsciously select which aspects of a situation to notice and which to ignore, this is known as selective perception. It is often based on past experiences, expectations, and motives. Someone with selective perception might have the tendency to forget or not notice what doesn't favor them. An example of this is visiting a store looking for red sneakers; you become more likely to ignore any other sneakers in the store.

Another more cognitively relevant example is how people have the tendency to see or hear what they want. For example, your friend tells you a compliment from her sister but also tells you the bad things she has said about you in the past. If you already believe her sister has it out for you, then you are more likely to take on board the bad and ignore the compliment.

Equally, if you are a positive thinker, you become more selective in what you see and accept in life. So, you actively go through your experiences seeking the good rather than selectively noticing the bad.

Perceptual Set Theory

The concept of perceptual set is the tendency to perceive or notice some aspects of the available sensory data and ignore others. Your motivations, expectations, current emotions, and cultural background influence it. In other ways, cognitive bias takes over your interpretation of things. For example, if your cultural beliefs don't permit living with your girlfriend or boyfriend before marriage, you might judge those who do. Ultimately, perceptual set theory is about seeing the world through the lens of what you believe, feel, and are exposed to.

The Influence of Social Norms

When people collectively decide what is acceptable and true, that collective understanding becomes the normal standard. Societal and cultural norms can shape individual perceptions, leading to conforming thoughts and behaviors that align with those norms. For example, gender roles were understood to be a social norm before the 21st century. It was the societal standard for men to work and women to stay home and nurture households. Though some still follow that status quo, many have created a new shared standard where men and women share responsibilities.

Social norms can influence individual mindsets. You can feel pressured to make certain decisions based on what the majority believes. Human brains are typically highly susceptible to promoting conformity; none of us wants to be the odd man out. That's why when the social culture is to compare ourselves to other people's social media lives, people will do anything to look good to others. This can be detrimental to the mind. However, choosing to follow positive thinking and immersing yourself in cultures where it is socially normative to think optimistically is beneficial.

Impact of Memory on Thoughts

It can be said that every thought is embedded in a memory. A single event can create thousands of thoughts that we can draw from (Leaf, 2022). Memories can be informational, which is when particular facts, associations, and data are stored. Other memories can be emotional, and these are feelings that surface from informational memories. Lastly, physical memories are embedded in sensory experiences from emotional and informational memories. All of the memories we have are inseparable from our thoughts.

Flashbulb Memories

Flashbulb memories are vivid, detailed memories of significant events that can disproportionately influence current thinking and perceptions about related future events. They are commonly a mixture of informational and emotional experiences. People who experience flashbulb memories usually do so in photographic detail. Therefore, they have no problem remembering details about their experiences.

Schemas and Stereotypes

Schemas are mental structures that organize past experiences, and stereotypes are oversimplified ideas about groups of people. Both can influence how we process new information and affect our thoughts and behaviors.

The Role of the Hippocampus in Memory and Thought

The hippocampus plays a critical role in forming new memories. It controls how information is stored in the brain, which affects the continuity of thought and the integration of past experiences into present thinking. Your memories are stored in the hippocampus, and this region of the brain also influences how recollection is transferred from short-term to long-term memory. The hippocampus also controls spatial navigation, which is how you process direction and the environment around you.

Memory, emotions, and many other cognitive experiences influence how you process things today. Any associations that have been created in your mind will make you more vulnerable to thinking one way over another. Fortunately, noticing these associations and understanding the psychology behind thoughts can help you proactively choose your mindset. You can be someone who has made negative associations all their lives, but recognizing that and actively making new associations can change the course of your life. It can also play a massive role in how you process and apply future information.

At this point, you might be wondering how you can start to transform negative associations into positive ones. Well, the next chapter covers that.

Chapter 3:
Transforming Negative Thoughts

Life can be filled with a series of things to worry about. Finances, health, and relationships are all among some of the things that can ignite worry in life. Worry can create rumination, which occurs when your mind stays stuck in one negative loop after another. Repetitive negative thinking then tends to catapult us into heaps of anxiety, stress, and low self-confidence. Transforming negative thoughts is the key to adopting positive thinking and preventing the above-listed issues. Occasionally, everyone has unhelpful thoughts, and that's normal. However, these thoughts can change your day's trajectory when they become repetitive.

Cognitive distortions are repeated patterns of unrealistic negative thinking. These distortions are faulty habits of thinking that make it difficult to feel good about ourselves and our lives. Fortunately, negative thoughts can be transformed into more helpful, beneficial patterns. This chapter will help you learn practical strategies for recognizing, challenging, and transforming negative thoughts to foster a healthier, more positive mind.

Identifying Negative Thought Patterns

Negative thought patterns involve assuming faulty thinking as truth, even without evidence to support it. You might think you know what someone is thinking, how they are going to behave, and the outcome of thinking that is impossible to predict. For example, "I am sure they don't value my input," "I am incapable of learning this," and "The worst thing is going to happen; I feel it." When your thoughts are rooted in negativity, it is common for you to view things as proof of something being wrong with you—even though there isn't.

In his research, Aaron Beck assessed depressed patients to explore the cognitive theory (Whalley, 2019). Later, he proposed cognitive behavioral therapy (CBT) strategies to help people override negative patterns of thinking. Learning about negative thinking patterns can help you start the journey toward positive thinking. You can practice recognizing negative thought patterns so you can understand and correct them.

Transformation begins the moment you realize what needs changing. Make an effort to observe your thought patterns to foster the mental shift that you need. Recognizing common negative thinking patterns such as catastrophizing, overgeneralizing, and personalizing can help you transform negative thought patterns for the better.

Common Cognitive Distortions

Faulty patterns of thinking are known as cognitive distortions. These distortions highlight the negative loops created in our minds as default, unhelpful thinking patterns. Distortions are automatic processes and typically happen when our brains take shortcuts to conclusions.

The underlying causes of cognitive distortion are commonly worry about the future, fear of what people think, and stress about situations. When faced with uncertainty or challenging situations, these emotions can arise in anticipation of future issues. Cognitive distortions can quickly lead to feeling overwhelmed and helpless in situations.

Several cognitive distortions prevent people from seeing the bright side of things and keep them fixated on negativity. However, negative thoughts don't have to cause an inevitable spiral downward in your emotions. Once you understand which cognitive distortions you are prone to, you can implement helpful strategies to change them. Below are a couple of examples.

All-Or-Nothing, Polarized Thinking

When you think one unfavorable way about a situation, you tend to get trapped in an "all-or-nothing" pattern.

This typically happens when you adopt one view of something, and it's usually detrimental to you. Due to its narrow nature of focus, all-or-nothing is also known as polarized thinking.

Someone with this cognitive distortion will view situations as absolutes. It's either everything is good, or everything is terrible; there's usually no in-between. Yet, life is full of gray areas where you can have a good experience marked by some unfortunate moments.

An example of all-or-nothing thinking is someone who is struggling to learn a new skill today, and because of that they think that they will *never* learn it. Another is having bad luck in a couple of romantic relationships and concluding that relationships aren't for you because you will *never* get someone to fall in love with.

The examples above take a very black-and-white approach, which is an example of polarized thinking. Instead, recognizing that you are learning a new skill, as in the first example, can help you see an alternative perspective. Also, in the second example, changing the all-or-nothing distortion looks like accepting the relationships that didn't work out but also recognizing that there are plenty of people in the world, and you are bound to find someone who gets you.

Jumping To Conclusions

Additionally, jumping to conclusions is a common cognitive distortion that many of us fall into without noticing. This distortion is also known as mind reading or fortune-telling because people often assume the role of predicting future outcomes. You might assume that someone will react a certain way (mind reading) or guess that an event will unfold in a specific manner (fortune-telling).

An example of jumping to conclusions by way of mind reading is, "I just *know* my professor will grade me low on that paper because of the conversation we had after class." There could be absolutely no truth to your statement, but you believe it anyway, not realizing how faulty that thought actually is. On the other hand, an example of jumping to conclusions by way of fortune telling is, "There's no point in inviting them because I'm sure they won't come." Both examples show your mind jumping ahead and creating narratives out of fear or other negativity. But that's not all.

Should Statements

Cognitive distortions can also happen in the form of "should" statements directed at yourself or the people around you. Such statements occur when you impose fixed expectations on yourself and others based on unhelpful beliefs. Should statements are typically made up of "must," "should," and "ought to" approaches to situations. For example, thoughts like, I was invited, so *I must, should, or ought to attend* can be detrimental.

Self-directed "should" statements lead to an internal experience of guilt, shame, disappointment, and anxiety. The same is true when such expectations are directed to others: "she must, should, and ought to" statements.

Whether we realize it or not, cognitive distortions tend to manifest and impact our emotional state.

Triggers and Context

Studies have found that cognitive distortions result from stressful life events, changes, and experiences that produce intense emotions and faulty thinking later in life (Pollock, 2023). Essentially, cognitive distortions are a result of preexisting biases that skew your way of thinking. Multiple contexts and personal experiences can evoke those inner biases.

For example, someone who was raised in a violent home (context) is likely to develop mistrust toward people in relationships. They are even more likely to feel strong emotions (trigger) in situations of confrontation.

The mind develops negative thinking patterns to protect itself. So, you might invite a few people to your home, but tell yourself that they won't come because you are less likely to feel disappointed if that negative belief turns out to be true. However, cognitive distortions can impact your relationships and responses later in life. You might even find yourself interpreting neutral events negatively.

Identifying situations, environments, or interactions that trigger negative thought patterns is helpful. It is better to anticipate the triggers and contexts that cause negative thinking so you can learn to manage these.

Self-Monitoring Techniques

Cognitive distortions start as automatic thoughts that develop into intermediate and core beliefs from the experiences you are exposed to. Intermediate beliefs include personal standards, attitudes, and assumptions. As your negative thinking patterns are reinforced over the years, these intermediate beliefs become core beliefs.

So, monitoring and intercepting your automatic thoughts early or identifying and unlearning your intermediate beliefs can prevent these negative thoughts from becoming core beliefs. Practical methods like thought records and mood journals can help you track your thoughts. Self-monitoring techniques help you identify cognitive distortions over time, enhancing self-awareness, emotional regulation, and control.

Thought Records

As a traditional approach to unlearning unhelpful thinking, thought records help people discover what they are constantly thinking and the visual representations they've created to support these thoughts. When the thoughts are clear to the person thinking them, it's helpful to unpack and trace them back to where they started to find balance.

Thought records are excellent for catching automatic thoughts. People who complete thorough records tend to notice significant differences in thinking patterns and their approach to life. In each thought journal, you are encouraged to write down your thoughts as soon as they come up so you can get to the root of why you thought that way to begin with.

Mood Journals

Document your thought patterns using mood journals to help you understand your feelings. Tracking your mood can give you insight into your thoughts since those affect how you feel and behave. Mood journals are powerful tools to increase self-awareness and cope with negativity. Keeping a mood journal allows you to process events and situations that negatively impact how you feel.

While you shouldn't stress about journaling your mood daily, being consistent is key to recognizing your thinking patterns and behaviors. Setting reminders for yourself to sit down and be intentional about journaling can help you make it a habit. Eventually, your mood journals will help you identify your triggers and patterns.

Consider assessing your goals with each mood journaling opportunity: What are you hoping to achieve? Give yourself a chance to focus on specific emotions and reflect on those triggers. Also, schedule daily reflections and reviews of your entries. Professional assistance offers a guided approach to self-monitoring and is also a good option to consider in your journey of changing negative thinking patterns. Below is an example of a thought record and mood journal table that you can use to make things easier for yourself. Use the first entry as guidance.

Mood and Thought Self-Monitoring Table

Day 1	*Situation*	I was leaving work and got a tire puncture.
	Thought	I'm stuck, and I don't even have someone to call.
	Emotion	Sadness, anger, and self-pity.
	Response	I sat in my car for a bit, then called my insurance to help with the tire issue.
	Future Recommendations	I need to start trusting my support system to help me in stressful situations; there's no need to feel alone when I have people who love me. So, next time, call insurance and a friend.

Day 2	Situation	
	Thought	
	Emotion	
	Response	
	Future Recommendations	

Day 3	Situation	
	Thought	
	Emotion	
	Response	
	Future Recommendations	

Day 4	Situation	
	Thought	
	Emotion	
	Response	
	Future Recommendations	

Day 5	Situation	
	Thought	
	Emotion	
	Response	
	Future Recommendations	

Monitoring your inner cognitive processes can offer a sense of relief. When faced with challenges, you naturally start to handle them more positively as you continue to work through the automated negative thoughts.

Understanding the Sources of Negative Thoughts

Exploring the origins of negative thinking, including past experiences, cultural influences, and environmental factors, helps you work through them. So, what are the sources of your cognitive distortions?

Influence of Childhood Experiences

Early life experiences and upbringing can set the groundwork for certain negative thought patterns, such as fear and self-doubt, and these can manifest in adulthood. Many people fall into the trap of cognitive distortions, and even children are susceptible. For example, when parents separate or friendships end, children can personalize those experiences as negative thought patterns. These cognitive distortions can affect mental health and interpersonal relationships in children.

Cognitive distortions in children are typically expressed through emotional reasoning, personalization, and all-or-nothing thinking. When children experience cognitive distortion, they jump onto an emotional rollercoaster.

Understanding that negative experiences and difficult upbringings can influence children in adulthood highlights the importance of addressing and changing these thoughts. Children coping with negative thinking patterns can be done by validating emotions, empathizing, and recognizing cognitive thoughts so that CBT techniques can be introduced early. Children need a safe space to grow, and those who don't receive that tend to have problems in the future as adults.

Cultural and Societal Conditioning

Cultural conditioning particularly involves traditions and values that are established over time within a community (Wilson, n.d.). You might behave a certain way every time simply because that's how things have "always" been done. On the other hand, societal conditioning refers to trends and shared beliefs that may not necessarily be assigned values, but people comply with them to fit in. Both forms of conditioning influence behaviors and perspectives. Societal norms and cultural backgrounds can shape your propensity toward negative thinking, and awareness of these influences can help overcome them.

Stress and Lifestyle Factors

Work pressure, a breakup, or financial problems are common stress triggers or stressors that can make you adopt negative thought patterns. Alongside modern life stressors, lifestyle choices such as lack of sleep, poor diet, and minimal physical activity can also exacerbate negative thinking. For instance, balancing family and work can affect your mind, body, and behaviors. However, identifying the stressors and lifestyle factors causing you to think negatively is a step toward change.

The Role of Self-Awareness in Thought Transformation

Self-awareness begins when you can face the thoughts that are keeping you in a negative thought cycle. Increased self-awareness can facilitate the positive changes you want to see in your negative thinking patterns.

Being self-aware allows you to trace your thoughts and monitor your emotions. This awareness can help you identify what patterns need changing and guide you to become a more positive thinker. Self-awareness enables you to reach the depths of your thoughts so you can gain sufficient knowledge to regulate your emotions, change your thoughts, and improve your behaviors.

Transformation through self-awareness enhances the quality of your life and social connections. There's power in knowing yourself deeply; that's why thought records and journaling matter, but you can also use mindfulness practices and other approaches to increase self-awareness. Let's take a look.

Mindfulness Practices

Mindfulness exercises can enhance moment-to-moment awareness, helping you recognize and pause automatic negative thoughts as they occur. Improving self-awareness through mindfulness can strengthen emotional regulation and help you focus on transforming negative thinking patterns.

Being mindful is the best gift you can offer yourself. It enhances your appreciation for what matters while reducing stress and negativity. The best part is that you don't have to dedicate chunks of time to practicing mindfulness. Instead, you can include it into your routine in the most simple ways.

Mindful Habits: Breathing, Eating, and Walking

Introduce mindful habits into your routine. Start with mindful breathing exercises, which are all about paying attention to the present and being aware of your breathing. The breathing process is easy to overlook because it comes naturally to us. However, with mindful breathing practice, you can learn to focus on your breathing as a tool to hone positivity and mindfulness.

Breathe deeply through your nose until you can't breathe more air in. Make sure that your abdomen rises as your lungs fill up with air. After that, exhale slowly and imagine stress leaving your body. Repeat this process as many times as you need until you feel relaxed. You can even place one hand on your chest and the other on your stomach while closing your eyes to maximize the experience. It's a simple yet powerful process that allows you to foster mindfulness and self-awareness.

Mindful eating is another habit that you can introduce into your daily routine. When you snack and eat meals, savor every bite. Avoid the temptation of sitting on your couch or watching television while eating. Instead, sit with your food and make it a habit to absorb the flavors, pay attention to the textures, and taste each enjoyable bite. Focusing on sensory experiences when eating helps you develop a deep connection with your body and an enjoyment of your food.

Eating mindfully is just the start; you can also include mindful walking daily. Make every walk you take a memorable one by taking your time with it. Embrace your surroundings and feel your feet touch the ground with each step. Mindful walking is about paying attention to every sensation that comes from doing something as regular as walking but intentionally and attentively.

Mindful habits foster a deep connection between you and your experiences. It's all worth it to keep those positive thoughts going.

Body Scan

Guide yourself through a body scan, which involves being attentive to each section of your body. Pay attention to what your body is telling you. Are there any aches or tensions? How can you breathe into this and allow yourself to release it? Body scanning is about letting go of tense or uncomfortable physical sensations. It's a way to enhance awareness by welcoming physical acceptance and relaxation.

Loving-Kindness Meditation

Loving-kindness meditation (LKM) is a mindfulness practice that focuses on positive actions and gestures of love toward you and those around you (Buzanko, 2024). The idea of LKM comes from ancient Buddhist customs, rooted in the belief that positive qualities and intentions boost emotional and mental health. You usually start with yourself so you can share loving kindness with others. For example, repeat a supportive phrase or statement to yourself daily. This sets the scene for you to become your own cheerleader in various situations. The more you can believe in your capabilities, the more you'll be able to support others as well.

LKM is about wishing yourself and others well and then acting in a way that proves this intention. Write love notes, see the best in people, tell yourself you can do hard things, and offer compliments. Your friends, family, and strangers can benefit from LKM just as much as you. It's a mindfulness practice that nurtures empathy, kindness, and compassion to foster mental resilience and positivity.

Enhancing mindfulness through practices of your choice improves your interest in life and people. Over time, you also develop a lot of empathy and gratitude. All of this enhances your experience as a person and adds value to your relationships.

Feedback from Others

Feedback from trusted friends or mentors can help you gain new insights into your thinking patterns. It gives you an advantage in identifying personal blind spots, supporting broader self-awareness. So, if you have people you trust, ask them to hold you accountable when you complain and also encourage you with constructive feedback that you can use to improve as a person.

Emotional Intelligence Development

Emotional intelligence is critical for understanding and managing emotions, as well as for changing deeply rooted negative thinking. When you are self-aware, you become better at identifying your emotions and working through the negatives. This increases your understanding of your strengths and areas that need improvement. So, emotional intelligence fosters self-awareness and allows you to keep growing.

Reframing Techniques

Now that you know how to identify negative thought patterns, reframing them into more positive, constructive perspectives is beneficial.

Cognitive Restructuring

Earlier in the chapter, we discussed CBT, which is heavily based on cognitive restructuring. It's all about changing the way you see things so you can transform your behaviors. Cognitive restructuring involves challenging and changing negative thoughts by focusing on evidence-based thinking and rational evaluation.

For example, taking the Socratic approach to processing negative thoughts will help you catch and change them. The Socratic approach to cognitive restructuring involves interrogating unhelpful ideas or emotions as they arise. You might ask yourself a series of the following questions:

- What am I concerned about?

- What do I think will happen?

- What will I do if my worst thought does happen?

- What does that matter?

- What triggered this way of thinking?

- Is there another explanation or likely outcome?

When you address your thoughts through a Socratic approach, you allow yourself to explore different, more positive ideas.

Perspective Shifting

Techniques for shifting perspective are essential. For example, viewing situations from someone else's viewpoint or considering the bigger picture can change your emotional responses. Your emotions can feel all-consuming. You might constantly fall into the trap of responding to intense situations emotionally. Perspective shifting is about seeing a situation from a healthy distance. For instance, think of what you would say or tell someone else to do if they were in your situation. Creating a healthy distance allows you to genuinely process the experience, be intentional about your responses, and make positive choices.

Use of Positive Affirmations

Positive affirmations can help slowly shift thinking from cognitive distortions to a more balanced or better outlook, reinforcing self-confidence and positive attributes. Affirming yourself is a way of removing your focus from the negative stuff to positivity. For example, "I am capable of completing essential tasks," "I can take breaks," "My energy is important to me," and "I am allowed to change."

You can personalize your affirmations to your situation. Personalized affirmations should feel like a friend reminding you of something positive in a moment when you need to hear it most. You should be that friend to yourself all the time. Speaking positively about yourself and your capabilities is uplifting and encouraging.

Let's switch things up a bit and explore the impact of your culture and bringing on fostering thought patterns. In the next chapter, we dive deeper into culture and environments to assess their relationship with thoughts.

Chapter 4:
The Impact of Culture and Environment

Your environment and cultural background immensely impact your mindset. Exposure to healthy settings can have a positive impact; the opposite is true of adverse situations. There's an intrinsic connection between mental health and your home, work, school, cultural, and social environments. Psychology refers to the places you are exposed to as factors contributing to your mental health.

Being aware of the factors that have psychological effects on you is beneficial in determining whether your environment is contributing positively to your mental health or to its decline. This awareness allows you to change your environment to shift your mental space. Recognizing when changes are needed helps you take actionable steps to become emotionally and mentally healthier. This chapter will help you examine how external influences like culture and environment shape your thinking patterns so you can navigate them positively.

Environmental Influences on Mindset

Environmental factors influence your mindset by altering your brain structure. Studies support the theory that people who grow up in adverse environments have slower brain development (Lindberg, 2023). When brain development is hindered, the risk of learning, memory, and behavioral difficulties increases.

Equally, people who are exposed to positive environments have healthy brain development. The areas you are in can raise or lower your stress. Your environmental setting either protects and equips your mind or opens the door to mental health struggles. Let's explore how physical environments impact mental states and thought patterns in urban and rural settings.

Urban vs. Rural Mindsets

At least half of the world's population lives in cities. Urban areas are commonly linked to mental health issues such as depression and schizophrenia. Urban environments, with their fast pace and high stimulus, can lead to stress and negativity. Loud sounds, clutter, and harsh lighting are primarily associated with urban spaces; these aesthetics can feel overwhelming and provoke anxiety. Urban living has a lot of rush that can cause social stress. Also, factors associated with urban spaces include air pollution and other toxins, limited greenery, crime, sensory overload, and social discrimination.

However, urban environments prioritizing social cohesion, security, and pleasantness tend to lower the risk of mental challenges. For example, living in gated communities can reduce exposure to crime, financial stability can reduce stress, and a strong family dynamic can increase happiness. So, living in a city can benefit mental health—for instance, access to transport, health care, quality education, and healthy social interactions.

In contrast, rural settings are more associated with healing properties. These areas promote a calmer, more positive outlook due to closer proximity to nature and less sensory overload. Rural environments offer a slower pace of living and allow for healthy solitude. People in rural areas are distant from traffic, pollution, and other issues.

However, rural areas can also present challenges. For example, it might be harder to travel between places due to a lack of infrastructure and resources and limited access to phones, healthcare, and other necessities.

Whether you live in urban or rural areas, finding ways to uplift yourself is imperative. In rural areas, take your time to appreciate the slowness of everything. Be mindful of what you have rather than constantly battling with what is lacking. Take time away from the noise in urban areas and find solace in the simplicity of green spaces.

Green Spaces and Mental Health

Green spaces are characterized by flowers, trees, grass, and open fields—so everything is nature. Access to parks and natural environments in urban areas can enhance mood, reduce stress, and support positive thinking. That's why some urban environments have dedicated areas to emulate green spaces, such as botanical gardens and rooftop gardens.

Nature has soothing effects. In Japan, a study conducted on 24 forests revealed that time in nature leads to lower heart rates, blood pressure, and stress levels (Hoge & Wulf, 2023). Simply reflecting on natural spaces during a walk, picnic, or quiet time does wonders for your mental health.

Design and Architecture's Role

Architectural elements like light, space, and room layout can influence mood and mindset, and optimizing living and working spaces can foster positivity. Design and architecture significantly affect how you feel, think, and behave. Dark spaces tend to inspire more negative responses compared to lighter environments.

The way buildings are structured shapes your experiences, emotions, and moods. The structure of environments can impact your entire well-being; for example, lack of exposure to sunlight and concisely living in a dark space can reduce joy and inspire feelings of helplessness. Alternatively, sunshine and bright spaces can make you feel motivated and determined.

When natural light comes into your lounge area, bedroom, or kitchen, it's shown to benefit mental health, reduce stress, and support your heart health (Fidanci, 2023). Buildings that have large windows, open spaces, skylights, and other aspects of natural light can make you feel more energetic and productive throughout the day.

Additionally, research shows that architectural designs with ecological connections can lower anxiety, enhance cognitive functions, and improve health.

Colors, textures, furniture placement, and so on influence your emotional and psychological state. When you choose vibrant colors for your homes, such as light reds, oranges, and yellows, it can promote energy and excitement. On the other hand, cooler colors, such as blue, green, and nude hues, can promote relaxation and calmness (Fidanci, 2023). Equally, textures and patterns add to your well-being and sense of comfort. Soft textures and soothing patterns create a level of familiarity and peace. In short, your environment and living space matter to your thought patterns; this includes your relationship with your family.

The Role of Family in Shaping Thoughts

Family dynamics and upbringing contribute to developing positive or negative thinking habits. An awareness of how family dynamics shape your thoughts allows you to move from negative patterns to conscious decisions (Foynes, 2021). Fortunately, you can decide which habit you can continue or let go of from your past. Identifying your early family patterns helps you focus on altering specific behaviors and habits from your family background. This offers new opportunities for self-reflection and development.

Modeling Positive Thinking

Parents and family members who model positive thinking and resilience can instill these traits in children, shaping their lifelong attitudes and mental resilience. Often, when we grow up in families that don't nurture our childhood needs, we grow up to become negative thinkers. However, we are better off when we experience positive, healing family dynamics. Parents need to model positive thinking to children because they grow up and adopt that behavior.

Communication Styles

Positive communication within the family, such as open expressions of affection, encouragement, and constructive feedback, builds a foundation for positive thinking. From a quick text to long-winded conversations with a fun friend, communication is key to positive thinking and building relationships. Personalities and perspectives also shape how you communicate.

Communication styles range from passive to aggressive. People tend to use four communication styles. One of these is passive communication, which means not speaking up but doing subtle things to get your message across. This type of communication can cause misunderstandings.

Passive communication is usually linked to fear, not positivity. On the other hand, aggressive communication is all about sharing your opinion and perspective regardless of how it affects someone else. Again, it's not really an effective way to communicate To combine these two, passive-aggressive communication, which appears as indirect communication, is expressed through negative emotions. It can cause confusion and resentment.

Alternatively, assertive communication is a confident, respectful way of communicating with others. It's usually regarded as the most positive and helpful manner of communication. Assertion is the consideration of others' feelings, opinions, thoughts, and beliefs. It promotes a safe space for conversions, regardless of opinion differences.

Handling Family Conflict

Handling family conflict requires strategies for managing and resolving issues to maintain a positive outlook and prevent the development of negative thought patterns. Learning ways to mediate is essential if someone in your family is aggressive, passive, or passive-aggressive in their communication. Also, learning healthy communication methods is beneficial if you are a negative communicator.

Firstly, it's essential to consider your relationships before you respond to anything during communication. Considering this gives you time to process the conversation before making any radical decision to respond and share your opinion. Remember, you love your family, so whatever you communicate needs to reflect that. So, take a step back if you need it and take your time to decide how to respond. Positive approaches are typically rooted in this consideration.

Also, active listening is a great way to handle family conflict. People want to feel heard and attended to; active listening promotes that. When you actively listen to someone, you allow them to share their post or view without interruption, and it's a positive way to get conversations and relationships moving. Positive communication strategies help you increase self-awareness, empathy, motivation, and self-control and improve empathy in relations.

Media Impact on Thought Processes

Media consumption, including news and social media, affects people's outlook and beliefs. Often, the media puts pressure on people to compare and doubt their achievements and capabilities to a lie. You learn to measure your successes with someone else's filtered accomplishments. However, the media can also have positive effects by helping you see where you belong. It's just important to balance your real life and the media's portrayal of how things should be.

Filtering Media Consumption

Critically assessing and filtering media consumption helps minimize exposure to negative content while promoting positive, uplifting content. Filtering your media consumption ensures that you avoid things that promote negativity and can instead focus on what adds to your life.

When you filter your media consumption, it enables you to concentrate on a drama-free life. You can filter your media consumption by following pages that align with the positive, good mindset that you want. Also, take breaks from social media occasionally so it's not the only source of support regarding how you should lead your life.

Balancing Awareness and Overwhelm

It's essential to stay informed but limit the risk of becoming overwhelmed with negative news. The contact influx of social media updates, news, and information can easily create sensory overload, making you feel hopeless and anxious about life. However, balancing awareness of what's happening in the world and taking time away from the overload can prevent feeling overwhelmed.

Positive thinking happens when you find balance in life, allowing you to remain hopeful and have a constructive perspective. You get to keep up with the world's current affairs because they affect you, but also decide how much time you spend getting informed by the news.

You can balance awareness and media consumption by scheduling when you'll watch the news, reading summaries, getting your information from positive spaces, and practicing selective reading. Sometimes, your mental health should focus on information that piques your interest. It's helpful to set media boundaries so you aren't overwhelmed by what you read online. Staying informed is essential, but it shouldn't come at the expense of your mental well-being.

Social Media as a Tool for Positive Connection

Social media can be a tool for positive connection if you let it. By filtering your media consumption and finding balance, social media can be a space for learning and support. You can use it as a way to connect to people who share similar interests and contribute positively to your life. Use social media proactively to build supportive networks and engage with content that enhances positive thinking and personal growth.

Socioeconomic Factors and Their Impact on Thought Patterns

Economic conditions and social class can influence your attitude (positive or pessimistic) and stress management. Socioeconomic factors include your income, what you have access to, and insurance. People who have access to all they need tend to experience less stress compared to those who need to fight for access. However, how much socioeconomic factors enrich your life also depends on your attitude. For example, a rich man can have everything money can buy but lack joy because they haven't learned to be content with what they have. Alternatively, someone with less could be happy with their life because they've learned to grow appreciation. Whether you are wealthy or figuring it out, economic stress is connected to your mental health.

Economic Stress and Mental Health

Economic hardship can lead to pessimism and stress, and strategies for maintaining a positive outlook despite financial stress are discussed herein. Money—or lack thereof—is reported as a significant stressor for most Americans (*Manage Your Stress in Tough Economic Times,*

2023). However, economic stress can be managed as you find a way to contribute positively to your mental health.

When you face economic stress, it's important not to panic. Regardless of what's on the news or online, don't get caught up in the doom and gloom of it all. Instead, focus on what you can do to improve your situation. For example, get a second job, invest what you can, and save. You can always take small, gradual steps to get to a better financial position. Your mental health will improve as long as you focus on positive thinking and actionable steps. Also, the source of economic stress must be identified, and a plan must be implemented to overcome it.

The Role of Community Support

Community resources and support networks in low socioeconomic areas are essential for fostering resilience and positive thinking. Community support can help you establish your plans and build resilience to economic stressors. If you find yourself feeling overwhelmed, the support of mentors, community leaders, and professionals can help you get back on your feet.

Social Mobility and Positivity

Financial strain and media influences can affect mental health. However, social mobility is the answer. It refers to improving your socioeconomic situation. When communities move together toward changing socioeconomic situations that future generations are born into, we inevitably prevent economic stressors for those coming after us.

The hope of social mobility influences positivity and motivation, helping you cultivate a helpful mindset to overcome socioeconomic barriers. Managing media consumption and social mobility are two of many ways to build positive habits. In the next chapter, we explore what it means to make positive habits.

Chapter 5:
Building Positive Habits

Brushing your teeth, fidgeting during a meeting, and putting your seatbelt on after you enter a car are all examples of habits you might have. Building habits is a process of practicing behaviors until they become automated patterns (*Habit Formation,* n.d.). Ultimately, habits are formed through repetitive action. Habits can be positive or negative, either benefiting or harming your life. When patterns in your life form with you consciously willing them there, you can actively change them to cultivate more positive ones.

You can build new positive habits by repeating them for several weeks. Every time you break a habit, you replace it with something else, so be attentive to what you are substituting daily habits with. This chapter helps you discover methods to develop new habits that reinforce positive thinking, ensuring these new mindsets stick long-term.

The Psychology of Habit Formation

We develop countless knee-jerk patterns as we navigate the world. Whether you are aware of your habits or not, you live them out daily. Your habits affect your behaviors, either helping you to meet your needs or distracting you from them. Since habits become deeply ingrained in behaviors, thinking, and responses, a process in our brains forms these patterns.

Habit formation is the brain's way of creating patterns to help you be more efficient. Your brain is constantly attempting to make things easier, so habits are formulated to prevent you from wasting time thinking about actions that you do continuously. The brain's tendency to push for efficiency can be a positive thing for us, especially when looking at helpful habits.

Understanding the mental processes behind forming and sustaining new habits is helpful in replacing unhelpful patterns with new ones. It's also great for dismantling habits that don't work in your favor. Habit formation can be harnessed to cultivate positive thinking; here's the logic behind this claim.

Neurological Underpinnings

Forming habits involves creating new neural pathways. Over time, these neural pathways become default stimuli for certain behaviors. Through learning and repetition, neural pathways are prompted to change and reflect your chosen pattern.

For example, negative patterns will cause neural pathways to change and create negative habit loops. Notice how you instinctively use a TV show to distract you from your textbooks? Well, that's because your brain has learned to associate your anxiety about studying with the pleasure of procrastinating through binge-watching Netflix.

Equally, repeating positive actions such as scheduling time for studying, regardless of how anxious you feel about staring at your textbooks, creates positive habits. Repeating actions influences neural pathways, demonstrating how consistent positive thinking can become automatic over time.

Reward Systems in Habit Formation

Reward systems are significant in forming new habits because they encourage the repetition of behaviors. There are multiple forms of rewards, from internal to tangible. The reward system can also be instantly gratified or delayed for long-term satisfaction. You can leverage the brain's reward system to reinforce positive habits.

For example, the feeling of satisfaction you get after completing a difficult task is an immediate reward. Alternatively, having to work an entire month to receive your next paycheck is a form of delayed reward.

Studies show that a balance between instant and delayed rewards helps us stick to certain habits longer. For instance, rewarding yourself with a healthy snack after a week of consistent exercise can motivate you to reach your fitness targets. Rewards are essential for habit formation because they are the gifts you give to yourself for your commitment to positive life changes. Rewards encourage you to continue in a positive direction.

Role of Trigger Identification

It is important to identify triggers that lead to negative habits and replace them with positive habits, which can lead to mental transformation and overall health. Triggers can be uncomfortable, but addressing them when they pop up is essential. People aren't meant to suppress emotions but to use them as a measure of what triggers us and how we can grow from it.

Triggers can also be caused by stress, which can cause poor habits and unhelpful behaviors. However, managing your triggers can help you be more intentional with your time and act in positive ways that enhance your experience.

Setting Up for Success

Habits are only formulated when behaviors are easy to engage with. It's less likely for your mind to lean toward a behavior if it's harder to do. For example, binging your favorite Netflix series is much easier to do than getting into the habit of covering the remaining workload. However, you can make this work in the future. So, if you know a negative habit is easy to do, perhaps making it harder for yourself can deter you from doing it next time. For example, if you have the habit of Netflixing instead of working, get your accountability partner to join you in a physical working session. This way, you'd be held accountable for working during the hours when you'd much prefer to Netflix.

Setting yourself up for success is essential. Create a conducive environment for positive habits, including organizing your physical spaces, having a routine, and scheduling. This can eventually help you cover the root of your habits and build more sustainable, positive ones. Adopting healthy routines and having a supportive environment will help you excel in the habit area. For you to thrive, forming positive habits through strategies that set you up for success is optimal.

Optimal Environment Design

Get into the habit of incorporating biophilic design into your environments. Designing your home and work spaces to emulate nature can encourage positivity. For example, plants and natural light elements can be included to reduce stress and promote mental health. Also, keep your spaces clean and decluttered to facilitate productive routines.

Routine Structuring for Positive Thinking

To start the day optimistically, bring structure into your life with daily routines. These should prioritize activities that promote positive thinking, such as meditation or positive affirmations. For example, wake up and say an affirmation to yourself repeatedly before reaching for your phone and getting on social media or checking emails. Start your day on a positive note that can carry into the rest of your experience.

Tools and Resources

Practical tools and resources, like apps or reminders, are helpful in creating an environment conducive to maintaining positive habits. So, get yourself acquainted with tools that will keep you motivated and hold you accountable for your daily goals. For example, *Streaks, Goalify,* and *Habitica* are great tools to help you build new habits and keep track of your progress. Using reminders or habit-tracking apps can help you stay motivated as you watch your habit formation progress into something beneficial.

Small Habits, Big Impact

The power of small, incremental changes in daily routines can lead to significant improvements in positivity. Your routine can be transformed into automatic patterns that help you throughout the day. For example, making drinking water before eating part of your routine will one day become a habit, which is something you do without thinking about it. Small habits create progress that becomes noticeable over time. The important part of habit formulation is welcoming the incremental approach to positive change; start and take one step at a time.

Incremental Approach

An incremental approach refers to the compound effect of small habits. It recognizes that minor changes like smiling more, breaking large goals down to doable tasks, or expressing small acts of kindness daily can gradually lead to significant positive shifts. Taking an incremental approach to transformation can positively change your outlook and interactions.

The Power of Mini Habits

To help yourself out even more, you can create mini habits by making incremental steps even smaller. The concept of mini habits, which are too small to fail routines, such as writing one sentence of gratitude each day, helps you form positive habits gradually. Mini habits are powerful in building confidence and developing a lasting positive mindset.

For example, someone who wants to start waking up early can make the change to wake up one hour earlier each week until they get to their target and can commit to it. Waking up at 11 a.m. might no longer be an option, so use one week to practice the mini habit of waking up at 10 a.m. daily. After that, wake up at 9 a.m. the next week, then 8 a.m. and 7 a.m. in subsequent weeks until you are happy with your time of choice. Slowly building new habits is better than sitting back and doing nothing at all to reach your goals.

Celebrating Small Wins

As you see progress in your life, it's essential to celebrate the steps you've taken to get where you are. Recognizing and celebrating small achievements can help you maintain motivation and bolster a positive self-image.

The Role of Consistency

Forming new habits is a journey of incremental habits coming together to make a big difference. Consistency is repeatedly doing something positive over a significant period (Rodriguez, 2023). It is crucial in habit formation and overcoming common barriers of procrastination and noncommitment. Being consistent each day ensures you create strong neural pathways to benefit your life over time. Consistency also creates momentum in your life, as your commitment reinforces constructive behaviors.

Overcoming Resistance

Procrastination and fear of failure are common psychological barriers to consistency, which can be overcome by focusing on the long-term benefits of positive habits. Being consistent with a habit helps you build resistance in the form of resilience. Your repetitive actions become a part of your daily routine. So, when negative thoughts and setbacks confront you, there are automatic positive patterns in your life to help you overcome them.

Building Resilience Through Routine

Consistent positive habits help build mental resilience, making it easier to revert to positive thinking even during challenging times. The rewards of your consistency are immeasurable. Over time, being consistent each day shapes your character and mindset. You begin to act through the lens of self-control, discipline, and confidence, leading to success in your life.

Accountability Mechanisms

In your journey of consistency, habit formation, and success, it's essential to remain accountable for your actions. Accountability ensures that you do things that keep you on track for fulfilling the goals you've set for yourself; this helps you cultivate a mindset of positivity. Setting up accountability measures, such as check-ins with friends or group support, helps you practice positive habits. For example, if you have a fitness goal, having a friend who's great at all things fitness and health as your accountability partner can remind you of your responsibility to continue positively in the direction of your goals.

Building positive habits is how you thrive in life and win in the face of adversity. The next chapter explores mastering resilience and overcoming adverse situations through positive thinking.

Chapter 6:
Mastering Resilience and Thriving in Adversity

Resilience is the evidence of overcoming setbacks and challenges in our lives. Many factors influence how resilient people become, including unique traits, the environment, and learning capacity (Sutton, 2019). You are more prone to building resilience if you are determined, in a supportive environment, and can learn to adapt to situations.

Resilient material can be stretched and bent various times and return to its original state after a while. Equally, resilience in the human context is about learning to be flexible so you can pivot or adapt to life's obstacles. Mastering resilience is about understanding that life won't be perfect. If anything, the most successful people in the world are the ones who are stretched and pulled in every direction but know to bounce back when they fail.

Of course, resilience goes beyond bouncing back from setbacks; it's also about creating effective strategies to help you cope with future challenges. Life's obstacles change you, whether you want them to or not. However, resilience ensures that you experience positive transformation to enhance your responses to future setbacks.

When you master resilience, you can overcome different setbacks and establish a renewed purpose. Over time, stress becomes easier to manage because your resilience reminds you that you can conquer whatever comes your way. This chapter uncovers the secrets to building resilience through positive thinking, enabling you to thrive even in the most challenging times.

The Components of Resilience

No matter how well-planned, plans can be disrupted. Instead of giving up when things don't work, resilient people permit themselves to grow through the difficulties. Resilience is about learning from mistakes and setbacks and not letting the bumps in the road deter you from achieving your goals. As such, components of resilience include flexibility and mental agility, perseverance, and positive thinking. Understanding what each of these components entails can motivate you to master resilience and thrive in adversity.

Flexibility and Mental Agility

Flexibility allows one to adapt to new situations quickly, making potential stressors manageable. For example, one could set a goal and realize that they overestimated its scope, and that's where flexibility comes in. Showing resilience through flexibility helps one reset the goal and rearrange its scope to get back on track. Essentially, flexibility is about focusing on what adjustments you are willing to make when the unpredictability of life happens.

It involves recognizing that your plan can change in the face of adversity, but your goal doesn't have to.

Resilience demands flexibility in thinking because there will be times when things won't go as planned, and you need to change your approach—and that's okay. Staying flexible keeps you adaptable, making it possible to learn new skills under pressure and thrive. You become even more of an unstoppable person when you can combine this flexibility with mental agility.

Mental agility at work includes thinking critically, problem-solving, making decisions, and leading confidently. Someone who is mentally agile knows how to process disappointments when setbacks come but just as quickly learns how to think of solutions to prevent future issues. Mental agility is a valuable skill that allows you to respond appropriately to setbacks and overcome them. When mentally agile, you are tenacious, determined, and gritty. You have no quit in you. Instead, you pause, reflect, put on your thinking cap, plan, and take steps toward your goal.

Perseverance Through Positivity

Life can be rough, and perseverance helps us maintain a sense of purpose by pushing through despite adversity. Preserving is action-based. It's about using your flexibility and mental agility to address issues with a goal. Merging your perseverance with positivity helps you forge forward positively, knowing your perseverance will pay off in time. Positivity enables you to push through challenges by motivating you to strive toward goals despite setbacks. As such, perseverance can be said to act as a buffer against discouragement.

True perseverance takes commitment and practice. It's like a muscle that you need to strengthen over time. The more you persevere in adversity, the stronger that muscle becomes. You can start from ground level, seeing every obstacle as an inconvenience. Then, over time, with perseverance and positive thinking, you begin to welcome the challenges. You start to see them as resources to refine your skills and make you better as life continues to promote you to new heights. Perseverance instills self-belief; it's remarkably empowering.

Positive Thinking as a Resilience Builder

Positive thinkers are happier and more resilient, viewing difficulties as temporary and surmountable. Everyone faces challenges at some point in life, and our approach to these challenges determines our personal life experiences. Positive thinking helps you build resilience and approach challenges in beneficial ways. Positive thinking involves building yourself up in the face of adversity. It fills you with self-confidence and the belief that you can overcome difficulties.

As a resilience builder, positive thinking balances your hopes to overcome adversity with practical steps to achieve the outcome. When you permit yourself to think positively about situations, you reframe the experience to enable you to face reality and focus on growth opportunities. Your mind becomes more resilient as you balance realism with positivity.

So, positive thinking plays a significant role in building resilience because it helps you face what is (the present) while embracing the beneficial possibilities of overcoming adversity. While maintaining a positive attitude isn't always smooth sailing, you can develop resilience through practice, focus, and dedication to positivity. By cultivating a positive mindset, you are equipped to face challenges and capitalize on every experience so you can thrive.

Psychological Traits for Thriving

The resilience components mentioned earlier in the chapter highlight some of the traits people need to thrive in the world. Thriving is about reaching new heights in development and various other life aspects. Human beings have always learned to survive and thrive in environments. Thriving predates the 21st century; it's a scientific phenomenon that can be observed dating back to the 60s or even earlier (Ziozas, 2021). Historically, humans have been known to have the innate motivation to self-improve and grow. So, it is no surprise that we carry psychological traits for thriving in our genealogy. In a sense, all human beings are hardwired to seek, chase, explore, and push toward thriving.

To thrive, it's helpful to embrace the following psychological traits: courage, adaptability, and emotional resilience. These traits are inherently connected to success and thriving in life. Without them, achieving milestones, adopting a positive attitude, and overcoming obstacles is unheard of. Let's take a deep dive into these psychological traits so you can understand their value and leverage them in personal experiences.

Courage to Face Uncertainty

Courage, bolstered by positive thinking, empowers people to face uncertainty, adversity, and risk confidently. It transforms fear into fuel that you can use to optimize every opportunity for growth. Courage provides a lens through which you can see good or bad situations as favorable parts of your learning and growing experience.

With courage, you become dedicated to putting your resilience into action and overcoming any obstacles in your way. A courageous mindset helps you see uncertainty as a clean slate for a new, uplifting story to be created. It enables you to take calculated risks and often reap the reward of your fearlessness. You are then eager to push limits, create new boundaries, and dare to succeed in many areas of your life.

Adaptability in Changing Circumstances

Another psychological trait for thriving is adaptability. This aligns with the components of resilience: flexibility and mental agility, whereby you can positively overcome challenges by finding solutions for them. Inherently, adaptability is about your ability to adjust to ever-changing situations.

Adjusting to different situations is a critical skill for your work and home life. Sometimes, you can plan the entire day to the last detail, but something deters your vision from materializing how you imagined. For example, you imagined waking up bright and early this morning, meditating just before relaxing with your cup of tea and going through emails just in time for your 10 a.m. meeting. Perhaps your alarm doesn't go off due to a depleted battery, and it throws a wrench in your calm morning plans. Suddenly, you wake up 15 minutes before your meeting, and all you can do is rush out of bed and look decent before it starts. A morning like this one can be chaotic.

However, adaptability allows you to pivot and let your frustration pass. It's about recognizing that the morning didn't at all turn out how you hoped. Equally, it understands that the rest of your day doesn't have to be tainted by that inconvenience. So, after your meeting, you can take a slow, warm shower, grab your tea, and return to creating the day you imagined. Adaptability requires you to make the most of the unfortunate aspects that life presents to you. This allows you to have a better experience tomorrow. For instance, you won't let the day repeat itself again because you'll know to charge your phone before bed so your alarm is ready in the morning.

Adaptability is rooted in a positive mindset. Consider adopting the approach, "Since this didn't work, what can I do for a better outcome next time?" Your ability to adjust hinges on accepting that things won't always go your way and understanding that you can use the setbacks as insight into what to avoid in the future. Adaptability helps people adjust their strategies and expectations in response to the unpredictability of situations. Due to adaptability, you become better at processing changes and pivoting to a new plan, thus maintaining your progress.

Impact of Emotional Resilience

Your ability to respond to daily stressors, emergencies, and crises is up to your level of emotional resilience. While you might feel stressed at moments, emotional resilience helps you get a sense of perspective. Instead of reacting to situations emotionally or having an outburst, emotional resilience allows you to pause and assess the problem before you respond.

Human beings live emotional lives that are shaped by personal beliefs and values; that's an understanding that dominates psychology (Heshmat, 2020). Much of what happens cognitively influences our physical experiences. Therefore, emotional resilience is important because it helps us regulate impulses to use our emotional cues more effectively.

Being emotionally resilient helps you put positive thinking into practice. You get to realize just how resilient you can be in the face of triggers and adversity. Emotional resilience makes it possible to accept the experience while working on helpful ways to manage it. Being emotionally resilient makes you a great leader, team player, and partner in work and home environments, enabling you to thrive. When you are emotionally resilient, you can make the best out of a bad situation, enriching your life in more ways than one.

Emotional resilience, supported by positive thinking, allows people to recover from emotional distress more quickly and effectively. Building emotional resilience helps you manage high-pressure situations by reducing stress and helping you view experiences through a positive lens.

Learning from Setbacks

A combination of emotional resilience, adaptability, and components of resilience all give you the advantage of learning from your setbacks. Remember, everything that doesn't work out as you hoped gives new insight for future plans. Setbacks help you adjust your approach to improve your chances of success and, viewing setbacks positively offers an opportunity for you to thrive.

Reframing Setbacks

Reframing is a way of coping with tough situations by viewing them from a more positive perspective (Sutton, 2019). Positive emotions can broaden your perspective and help you create alternative solutions for setbacks. Reframing lets you see problems as solvable rather than insurmountable obstacles. It helps you improve your sense of capability, boost creativity, and enhance your ability to connect with supportive people in a solution-making process.

Reframing your situation can help you build self-confidence, establish a strong sense of self-esteem, and be more cooperative in situations that need solutions. Over time, you learn to manage stress and actively engage in meaningful experiences. Reframing also helps you recognize that setbacks are temporary, helping you feel a deep sense of hope as you tackle different challenges.

The Art of Reframing: View Setbacks as Feedback

You can reframe your setbacks by seeing each one as feedback. As stated earlier, think of your experiences, good or unpleasant, as research for the future.

Your successes show you your strengths and capabilities, while setbacks teach you what you can improve. Viewing setbacks as feedback allows you to reflect on new approaches to situations, reframe your perspective, and adapt.

When you become familiar with reframing, you develop problem-solving, goal-setting, effective communication, emotional intelligence, and many other valuable skill sets. Your mindset goes from "This sucks" to "This is a valuable lesson that I can use to thrive in future challenges." The art of reframing by viewing setbacks as feedback contributes to your success.

Positive Feedback Loops

Feedback is a valuable aspect of personal growth. It helps you learn and adapt to situations. When you receive feedback, it either motivates current behavior or demonstrates the need for improvement. We've touched on how reframing is seeing feedback as a demonstration of improvement, and the alternative to that is positive feedback loops, which promote helpful behaviors.

For example, parents will use positive feedback to get their children to continue desired behaviors, such as offering healthy rewards for good behavior or even praise for a job well done. The same approach can be effective in adulthood.

During setbacks, focusing on your strengths, contributions, and value through positive feedback can help you reinforce positivity. When you notice what you are good at in tough times, you become self-compassionate about what needs improvement. For instance, say you take a test and do really well in one section but terribly in another; rewarding yourself for the part you aced while recognizing what needs improving helps you keep a positive attitude.

Instead of thinking, "I'm bad at everything," you begin to notice, "Oh, I'm good at this, and if I can improve this section, I'll be even better." Maintaining a positive outlook when confronting setbacks creates a feedback loop over time where each obstacle you face enhances your learning capacity and future performance.

Setbacks as Windows of Opportunity

Recognizing that seizing every moment is key to mastering resilience and thriving will help you build on your life experiences. A window of opportunity is the ability to positively consider every experience as a favorable chance to create change in your life.

Think of setbacks as periods in time where you are given a chance to either grow or shrink back and let life overwhelm you. People who see things from a positive thinking perspective can tackle setbacks with a growth mentality. You've got to say to yourself, "If life is going to happen, I choose to believe it's happening *for me*, not to me." When you adopt positive thinking this way, you climb into that window of opportunity, and on the other side, you thrive!

Viewing setbacks through a positive lens, where each misstep is seen as a stepping stone to mastery and personal growth, promotes a more resilient mindset. Setbacks are not to stop you from thriving but to push you to master resilience and overcome adversity.

Remember, setbacks don't influence the final outcome; your response to setbacks does.

Prepare for a Positive Outcome: Adopting a Growth Mindset in Adverse Conditions

A fixed mindset causes many cognitive distortions, so adopting a growth mindset is essential. While a fixed mindset makes you see things in one way or another, good or bad and all-or-nothing, a growth mindset allows room for numerous possibilities. It can help you view difficult situations in hopeful, positive ways. Yet, a fixed mindset can keep you stuck in old and unhelpful patterns, increasing frustration in your life.

Embracing mistakes and acknowledging your weaknesses as personal advancement opportunities is integral to a growth mindset. It's all about accepting where you've fallen short so you can use those setbacks to propel you forward. Adopting a growth mindset in adverse conditions prepares you for a positive outcome. Let's take a look at how.

When Challenges Become Opportunities

Fueled by positive thinking, a growth mindset allows people to view challenges as opportunities to strengthen capabilities and improve knowledge. A growth mindset views challenges as resources that sharpen your skills and develop you over time. Your willingness to let challenges become opportunities leads to mastery.

In the face of challenges, a growth mindset says, "This challenge is difficult because I am still developing my skills in this area." This contrasts with the fixed mindset, which states, "This challenge is difficult because I am naturally horrible at it." Challenges threaten a fixed mindset because it sees absolutely no room for improvement. However, a growth mindset sees challenges as opportunities for personal development. You can adopt the growth perspective by letting go of rigid ways of thinking, reframing challenging situations, and bringing your positive thinking into play.

Continual Learning and Adaptation

Positive thinking motivates ongoing personal and professional development. This means you need to continuously adapt, take feedback, and see everything as a chance to learn. Continuous learning and adaptation involve viewing all feedback as positive, persisting through difficulties, and realizing that life constantly offers us opportunities to learn.

If you are learning, you are winning and developing new skills. So maintain a growth mindset and embrace the journey of continual learning.

Resilience Through Learning

Consistency, positive thinking, and being open to continual learning are essential to building resilience. If you think about it, you learn whenever you are faced with a situation that needs solutions you haven't considered before. You also learn when you embrace life's setbacks and unpredictable nature, which inspires critical thinking about subsequent plans. Every corner of life is a learning curve, and resilience develops every time you embrace those lessons.

Adopting a growth mindset contributes to resilience by enabling people to recover from adversities and grow stronger. Of course, positive thinking, laying the groundwork for success, and other psychological tools take time to learn. You need to be open to embracing the continual learning process that is life itself. Be patient as you harness the power of positive thinking. Mastering resilience takes time; it's not an overnight process. So give yourself ample time and compassion as you adapt to changing situations.

Think positively because it's empowering. Positivity develops your approach to life and helps you conquer challenging situations. Positive thinking also influences the quality of your relationships. The following chapter explores that.

Chapter 7:
The Role of Positivity in Relationships

Your attitude, positive or negative, is contagious. Most people prefer to be in relationships with people who have a positive mindset. Hanging out with positive thinkers brings happiness into spaces, and positivity motivates people in situations. Spending time with people who complain, only have negative things to say, make everything a self-pity contest, and are grumpy is not fun. That's why positive thinking is crucial in building strong connections with people.

Positive interactions can benefit both professional and personal relationships. Research shows that positivity is key to good relational outcomes. At work, positive thinking leads to greater negotiation, collaboration, and brainstorming abilities. It's equally beneficial with friends and family at home because positivity leads to mutually respectful conversations, active listening, and trust.

Positivity has a significant role to play in relationships. It can help you get along with people and make more friends because having a positive outlook on situations makes you far more likable. When it comes to creating strong bonds with people, positivity is non-negotiable. Your positive demeanor can cause people to gravitate toward you, putting them at ease. This is a win for your future as it helps you build valuable networks wherever you go, which can become great for your career and personal life. This chapter investigates how positivity can transform your relationships through approaches such as positive communication, empathy, and connection, which are the glue to social connections.

Foundations of Positive Interactions

Any true friendship or connection is built on positive interactions. When people have mutually enjoyable encounters, they typically walk away feeling satisfied. Learning the foundations of positive interactions can help you strengthen your current relationships and build new ones down the line.

Principles of Positive Communication

Positive communication is based on mutuality, so it's a two-way street. People who communicate positively can disagree but show consideration for someone else's perspective. Positive communication respectfully welcomes differences and can find common understanding between parties to ensure that each person's point of view is recognized.

During a conversation, each person should feel heard, valued, and appreciated. Positive communication requires shared participation through active listening, understanding, and observation. The people involved need to verify and validate how the message is being received and understood. Positive communication inevitably builds trust and mutual understanding.

Principles like respect, openness, and honesty are the bedrock of positive communication.

Respect

Positive communication requires consideration, which is the primary mark of respecting someone. Think about how you want people to communicate with you and do to others what you would be okay with them reciprocating. Extending respect looks like asking instead of commanding people to do stuff, valuing someone else's opinion even if it's different from yours, and letting others express themselves without interruption. Respect is an integral principle of positive interactions. The conversation won't go anywhere helpful without respect.

Openness

If we treat respect as a conversation starter, think of openness as the authenticity that keeps the conversation going. Openness is about expressing your thoughts, feelings, and understanding of the situation constructively and respectfully. Communicating openly with people demonstrates a level of trustworthiness that allows them to receive your vulnerabilities and share their own. Deep connection and understanding can't happen without openness. You need to be transparent to help people recognize that you are speaking truthfully and take you at your word.

Honesty

Openness and honesty go together. There's no point in being open if you're going to lie during a conversation. Positive communication is built on the ability to trust what someone is saying and develop your bond based on that. Honesty is an essential principle of positive communication because it fortifies the connection between people, making them secure in their interactions and relationships.

Positive communication is a brilliant way to show confidence in others and assertiveness in your message. It carves out positive interactions that can lead to successful, long-term relationships.

Role of Positive Language

Strengthening relationships through positive communication also involves the use of positive language. What you say and how you say it impacts how the message is received during conversation. Positive language ensures that the next person can feel your respect, see your honesty, and embrace your openness as you communicate. It increases the chances of understanding, cooperation, and proactivity among people. Positive language can influence interactions, setting a constructive tone that encourages connection and growth.

Framing your message using positive language significantly impacts interactions, leaving all parties feeling good. It's not just about using positive words but also about ensuring that the intention of your message is received through your delivery. Sometimes, it's tough to know if we are using positive language or not. Below is a summary table highlighting key differences between positive language and unhelpful language to help you make the distinction.

Positive language	Unhelpful language
It's helpful, reassuring, supportive, and empathetic.	It sounds much like blaming, shaming, or judging.
Informs the next person of what to do.	Tells the next person what *not* to do.
Provides the next person with choices and alternative options.	Doesn't provide options or alternatives.
It's crystal clear and promotes action.	It's passive, aggressive, or both.
It's encouraging.	It's restrictive and limiting.
It's responsive and constructive.	It's reactive and uninvolved.

Positive language should be an informative way to deliver a message, whether during an internal dialogue or with others. When language is used positively, it affirms, encourages, creates emotional security, and promotes positive interaction. You can use positive language daily to improve your self-image and relationships.

Feedback Loops in Communication

Positive interactions involve people having a chance to ask questions, share perspectives, and clarify misunderstandings. Since communication is a two-way street, it's essential for everyone participating to deliver a message, respond, feel validated, and receive confirmation to facilitate a feedback loop. So, positive interactions reinforce feedback loops, where kindness and positivity lead to more of the same, fostering a warm and supportive relationship environment.

Communication Skills for Positive Engagement

People create feedback loops in conversations by developing communication skills for positive engagement. Sharpening your skills takes practice, determination, and effort. Even so, as long as you remember openness, honesty, and respect, you are almost ready to take on a positive conversation. Communication skills help you ensure that the principles listed above are upheld. Active listening, effective affirmations or validation, and constructive feedback are essential for positive engagement. Let's unpack these techniques you can use to facilitate helpful dialogue.

Active Listening Techniques

Studies indicate that 65% of all communication is nonverbal, and knowledge of this will help you become an effective listener (Cunic, 2024). Active listening involves hearing words and understanding emotional undertones. It is essential for positive communication and creating a supportive dialogue environment. Active listeners listen more and talk less, are attentive to responses, ask relevant questions to facilitate understanding, avoid assumptions, and pause when someone else is talking to prevent interruptions.

Actively listening to people involves being attentive to both verbal and nonverbal messages. So, listen to what people are saying as well as what they aren't. Nonverbal language is expressed through facial expressions, body cues, and gestures. Someone might verbally express agreement about something by saying, "Yes, sure," and follow that up with nonverbal language such as nodding. In this case, both verbal and nonverbal expressions communicate their agreement.

However, there are instances when nonverbal language can tell you more about how a person genuinely feels beyond what they are saying. For example, someone might verbally communicate that they aren't upset about something but shrug at something you say. This can be a nonverbal clue that they might need a moment to cool off.

Essentially, being attentive to both verbal and nonverbal language can help you become an active listener. Consider the most recent example: noticing the shrug makes it possible for you to ask relevant questions to facilitate more open, positive communication that leads to a resolution. Yet, had you not noticed the nonverbal clue, the conversation would have ended with the person still feeling upset about the topic. Active listening creates conversational awareness that brings people closer.

Active Listening In Practice

So, now you know what active listening is all about, it's time to put it into practice. Below are quick tips that you can take with you into a new conversation.

An active listener

- is mindful and fully present in conversations.

- maintains good eye contact to show interest in what's being said.

- asks relevant questions to encourage further clarification.

- withholds judgment, assumptions, and unsolicited advice.

- paraphrases to understand the message ("If I'm hearing you correctly, you are saying...").

- prioritizes both verbal and nonverbal messages.

Being an active listener is crucial for maintaining healthy relationships. Active listening creates mutual understanding and ensures people are on the same page, enhancing how you relate.

Effective Use of Affirmations

Affirmations, which tie into active listening, help people feel heard and understood during conversations. They can also be used to reinforce positive behavior and strengthen relationships by communicating empathy. For example, if a friend has just finished telling you about a huge achievement, responding in a way that affirms this can be, "Wow, that's remarkable news. I knew you could do it. I'm so happy for you." First, you acknowledge the message, then you affirm their capability, and you share how you feel about what's been communicated.

Other affirmations can include the following:

- "I'm sorry to hear that, and I can see why it has upset you."

- "Your perspective is valid. If I had known my actions would make you feel this way, I wouldn't have done what I did."

- "You are such a great friend. Thank you for chatting with me."

- "I hear you, and I might not agree, but I respect where you are coming from."

- "It's always good to express yourself, and it helps me understand your needs."

Affirmations are essentially about validating what someone has communicated. This way, you and the speaker feel like active and respected participants in the conversation.

Constructive Feedback

Communication is more than affirming and listening to the next person; it's also about offering constructive feedback. Constructive feedback strengthens relationships and helps people develop. You can give constructive rather than critical feedback, using positive thinking to frame your suggestions. The aim is to encourage growth and improvement without causing defensiveness.

For example, "I appreciate your effort toward the group project. Your contribution to this work is invaluable. After reading the final section, I noticed that____ could use a bit more information about____ to make the work stand out more." It's good to point out what someone is good at and what you value before advising on what needs improvement. It's also practical to suggest alternatives of how someone can improve so they don't feel totally lost for options. When your feedback is given constructively, the other person will usually feel encouraged, not deflated.

Constructive feedback should help you and others reach a positive outcome after communicating. It usually leads to improvement in behaviors, approaches, and perspectives.

Building Emotional Intelligence

Building emotional intelligence greatly benefits your relationships. Being emotionally intelligent means you can recognize your emotions and the role they play in your behaviors. Building emotional intelligence involves addressing the primary areas of self-regulation, awareness, and empathy development. People with high emotional intelligence are typically stronger in these areas than those on the lower end of the scale.

High emotional intelligence makes it possible to practice self-control in situations where you'd much prefer to respond with negative impulses. It also helps you become more empathetic toward others and aware of the responsibility you have over your actions. The components of an emotionally intelligent person make it possible to harness the power of positive thinking, even in the most demanding situations, strengthening your relationships with others.

Self-Regulation and Emotional Responsiveness

Self-regulation is a vital component of emotional intelligence. It is when people can manage their emotions, allowing them to stay calm, mindful, and positive. The ability to self-regulate makes it possible for you to be more responsive rather than reactive in situations, influencing personal and professional interactions positively. Self-regulation is marked by positive characteristics such as thoughtfulness, integrity, and respect, which are wonderful for sustaining relationships.

Empathy Development Practices

Empathy is the second most crucial component of emotional intelligence (Mind Tools Content Team, n.d.-c). This is sharing and understanding other people's emotions, needs, and perspectives. Empathetic people recognize other people's emotional experiences and can avoid passing judgment.

Practices to develop empathy include perspective-taking exercises and empathetic listening. These are great tools for enhancing understanding and deepening connections in relationships. Empathy is foundational to building relationships because it helps you relate to the human experience. So, you become better at communicating openly and more honestly.

Emotional Awareness in Communication

Being aware of your emotions and those of other people is another key aspect of emotional intelligence. Emotional awareness helps communication to be more effective and positively received. When it comes to communication, emotional awareness tends to be misunderstood.

Being emotionally aware is different from emotional regulation. The latter is about maintaining authority over how your emotions manifest in behavior. On the other hand, emotional awareness is about knowing and understanding what you are feeling so that you can begin the regulatory process.

Understanding your feelings can help you communicate successfully with others. Emotional awareness in communication makes it possible to articulate your needs and prevent confusion through conversations. Being emotionally aware also means you have a greater grasp of other people's feelings, allowing you to notice and respond to nonverbal cues appropriately.

You can also improve your emotional awareness skills by being more considerate of how others are feeling. Actively practice empathy and active listening to ensure that others feel cared for in conversations with you. Equally, consider your own emotions. How you feel can influence how you interpret what someone else is communicating, and it can shape how you view situations.

When you feel strongly about something, be attentive to that feeling. Process what the emotion signals to you are and do your best not to judge or try to change the feeling. All emotions are integral to your approach to relationships, so taking your time to be more aware of them is essential.

Emotional awareness improves how you interpret conversations, allowing you to process other people's perspectives effectively. This awareness makes sharing in deep connections and healthy discussions possible, helping each person understand what the other is communicating and why.

Impact of Positivity on Conflict Resolution

Though the objective of any positive communication is to prevent arguments by understanding where people are coming from, sometimes conflicts are unavoidable. However, if they are dealt with positively, conflicts can benefit relationships. That's where conflict resolution comes in.

Conflict resolution is about managing differences in perspective in positive, constructive ways. It involves using positive language and observing the principles of positive communication so that disagreements can be turned into learning opportunities. Learning to manage disputes through conflict resolution can improve your professional and personal relationships, increasing the frequency of positive interactions.

Embracing conflict in your relationships gives them a chance to grow stronger with more understanding and empathy. People are unique, so we are bound to have differences in opinion. The positive way to approach those differences is with respect and curiosity. Instead of suppressing opinions or avoiding disagreements, it benefits everyone to face them positively. Conflict resolution consists of active listening, affirmations, collaboration, and sharing ideas, all in an effort to reach common ground.

Transforming Conflicts with Positivity

Maintaining a positive outlook during conflicts can help transform potentially volatile situations into constructive discussions. Bringing a positive attitude to conflicts enables you to focus on solutions rather than problems, allowing for resolution to happen.

Transforming conflicts with positivity enhances trust, builds rapport, and fosters collaborative problem-solving. Approaching disputes with a shared and positive outcome transforms the quality of interactions. It also allows for constructive feedback, relationship satisfaction, and positive engagement to continue. But where do you begin transforming conflicts into positivity? Well, start with positive thinking.

Agree There's Conflict

When conflicts arise, frame them as a chance to learn from someone else's perspective. So, enter the conversation first to agree that a conflict needs addressing. This means don't cast blame or take blame; instead, focus on the situation. Conflicts aren't about people but about perspectives. Therefore, agreeing that a misunderstanding is happening will help you transform conflicts with positivity. The issue isn't you or the other person; the issue is the tension between you.

Explore Differences and Similarities

Once that agreement is reached, you can move on to resolving the tension. Start by highlighting each person's perspective and what each person understands from the moment. Then, attempt to point out similar and different perspectives. Similar perspectives help you see that there are some things that you agree on, which offer hope for resolution. The differences, however, highlight areas that might be causing tension and need to be addressed. Use that information to start brainstorming mutually beneficial solutions.

Create Common Ground

Talk about how you differ in perspectives and why. The objective isn't to bicker in an attempt to change someone's mind or impose beliefs on the next person. Instead, it's to identify the areas of concern so you can either see why someone could interpret things a certain way or agree to disagree and move on amicably.

Reach a Resolution

Once you've taken the time to listen to one another and respect varying perspectives, put the issue to rest. Conflict resolution happens when the parties involved can reach a mutual solution on how to move forward. It doesn't always mean that perspectives change. Instead, everyone has agreed to focus on a positive outcome.

Preventative Positivity: The Role of Optimism in Resolving Disputes

Optimism can play a crucial role in conflict resolution. It drives the belief that a beneficial resolution is possible, motivating continued engagement and problem-solving. Adopting a consistently positive approach in interactions can prevent many conflicts from arising by reducing misunderstandings and fostering a climate of cooperation and mutual respect.

Optimism and positivity can be resources to prevent conflict from escalating. An optimistic attitude allows one to remain levelheaded, patient, and kind during conflict. Positive thinking impacts your mind, relationships, perspective, and how you approach the future. The next chapter explores the concept and practice of visualization as it pertains to using your mind to create what you want to see.

Chapter 8:
Visualization and Goal Setting

Visualization techniques are misunderstood as mystical and unrealistic but are more grounded in reality than any other technique. You don't have to be spiritual or a master manifester to use visualizations in your favor. The practice of visualization involves creating a mental image of your future achievements. It's all about using your senses, ambitions, imagination, and actions to realize your goals.

It's helpful to apply the principles of psychology: positivity, consistency, and helpful behaviors to actualize your hopes and make visualization work. Visualizing trains your mind to respond to situations and your current life as if your mental image is true. This chapter will help you learn to harness the power of positive thinking through visualization. The objective is to clarify and achieve your goals, linking positive thinking with concrete success.

Basics of Visualization

Visualization allows you to direct your mind to set parameters for future success. It's about concentrating on what matters most to you and achieving it. When you visualize, you participate in selective attention, focusing only on things that will help you achieve a desired outcome.

Visualization basics involve maximizing your cognitive functions, considering the psychological impact of visualization, and consistency. You don't just visualize what you want once, but it's done a number of times until it becomes habit. Visualizations draw you closer to achieving what you want in life because they keep your mind focused on the positive outcome of the things you imagine. So, no distractions or negative thinking can overwhelm you as you work toward what you've envisioned.

Neurological Basis of Visualization

Like positive thinking, visualization leverages the brain's neural pathways. As you envision what you want for yourself, your belief in receiving it grows, So, over time, you naturally focus on moving toward achieving the vision. When the brain's neural pathways are leveraged, visualization simulates real-life actions and prepares your mind and body to act as envisioned. This, in turn, enhances the likelihood of achieving the visualized outcomes through positive reinforcement.

Psychological Impact

The psychological benefits of visualization include higher motivation, enhanced self-confidence, improved productivity, and a positive mindset, which is crucial for achieving long-term goals. Additional benefits include memory, planning, and motor control improvement. You tend to be much happier and more focused when you visualize outcomes. When you achieve your vision, you feel a new sense of determination and drive to keep pursuing your goals. Visualization leads to fulfillment and overall positivity.

Visualization as a Habit

Ultimately, when you visualize, it's like rehearsing movements you already anticipate. When you think something, it activates the part of your brain responsible for exertion, making it possible to act on your thoughts or internal beliefs. Over time, your rehearsals through visualization inspire a routine of simple actions (habits) to achieve what you've envisioned. Making visualization a regular practice can transform it into a habit that continuously fosters positive thinking and goal orientation.

Types of Visualization Techniques

Turning visualization into a daily habit takes practice, effort, positive thinking, and time. It can be difficult to know where to start if this is your first time visualizing. Fortunately, visualization techniques are straightforward and can help you learn how to turn this beneficial practice into a daily habit you enjoy. There are plenty of visualization techniques to choose from, and this book covers guided imagery, a vision board, and mental rehearsals (repetition). These are all techniques you can incorporate at any part of the day to help you stay on track and visualize your goals successfully.

Guided Imagery for Specific Goals

Guided imagery involves creating detailed and controlled mental images to visualize achieving specific goals. It enhances focus and detail-oriented thinking to help you specify what you want and the action plan to get there.

The guided imagery technique for visualization is often used to reduce stress, enhance relaxation, and calm the mind. Guided imagery improves overall well-being and provides a sense of being grounded in this ever-busy world (West, 2022). Using guided imagery for specific goals helps you work your way toward achieving them.

For example, get into a comfortable position, whether sitting or lying down. Close your eyes and imagine achieving the goals that you've set for yourself. Envision what getting that promotion looks like and how it would feel. Take a couple of deep breaths so you can settle into the positive imagination of accomplishing an incredible career goal. Allow yourself to add more details to your mental image as you feel your feet on the cold office floor, hear your colleagues applaud, and notice each one smiling your way. Once you've absorbed that vision and its positive feelings, gradually open your eyes and bring yourself back to this amazing life you have. Take a peek at your vision board and start working on the projects you need to fulfill for that vision to come to fruition.

Guided imagery isn't just a form of visualization that draws on future goals. Instead, it's also about bringing reflection and relaxation into a moment by imagining your most peaceful place. For example, if you just came out of a stressful meeting, take two minutes to yourself to practice some guided imagery. You can sit on your office floor or in a chair and imagine you are at your favorite place to unwind. For some, this place is home on the couch, while for others, it may be at the beach. Say yours is the latter; imagine being by the ocean. Feel the sand hug your toes as you walk on it. Envision the clear sky, sun, sea breeze, and trees swaying. Do your best to engage your senses in every aspect of your vision. What do you hear? How do you feel?

With guided imagery, it's essential to allow your kind to be transported to a place where there is only positivity. If you aren't the best at focusing on one thing for specks of time, you can include guided audio or videos from YouTube. This way, you don't have to guide your own image but can listen to someone else guide you through the process.

Vision Boards to Sustain Motivation

Vision boards are motivational tools that align positive thinking strategies and detailed steps to create an actionable plan for what you want to achieve. Creating and using vision boards as a physical representation of your goals becomes a constant reminder of what you want to achieve. As the Dalai Lama once said, "In order to carry a positive action, we must develop here a positive vision" (Naylor, 2016). This quote, on its own, highlights the importance of having a positive vision as the foundation for future success.

Your vision board can consist of a collection of cut-out images or digital photos that map out what you want for your future. For example, if you envision graduation as a future goal, you can cut out magazine photos and stick them on cardboard pieces. Then, you can frame it as a reminder of graduation, so every time you are studying, you have the physical representation of what all the hard work is for.

However, since we live in a digital age, a digital vision board may be your go-to. You can create a Pinterest account and different boards that reflect what you want for each area of your life. Using images, outline personal goals for your relationships, academics, career, and so on. Pinterest is a great start! You can even print out each digital board once you are happy with it and plaster it in your home as a physical reminder of your intentions for yourself.

Visualization keeps you focused on your goals. Vision boards are tools to keep that focus alive and encourage motivation. It's great to place your vision board somewhere you frequent so you can see it daily. When your goals are in your face, they serve as instant and continuous reminders of your path.

Mental Rehearsals for Skill Enhancement

Athletes and performers use mental rehearsals to practice skills in their minds. Mental rehearsals are essential and rooted in repetition. You see what you want to see happen as though it already has, which helps improve actual performance by mentally simulating the steps needed to succeed. For example, a coach will say, "Fellas, we are not too far from winning this thing! Think about holding the trophy and impressing your family at home (guided imagery), now go out there to win! Say *win* on three..." and the athletes will follow the instruction. Mental rehearsals reinforce the "practice makes perfect" concept within a positive framework. You get to see the goal, envision your victory, and go out and make it happen. After all, you are far more prepared for your successes than your mind wants to trick you into believing.

Incorporating Visualization into Daily Routines

To start any visualization practice, it's important to get into a quiet spot where you can avoid distractions and unimportant interruptions. Incorporating your senses (smell, touch, hearing, and vision) into your visualization practices can help make the outcome feel more real.

Also, be patient with yourself and try not to rush the process.

Morning Visualization Routines

Start the day with a short visualization session to set a positive tone. Maintain a clear focus on your goals for today, integrating positive thinking right from the morning. Projecting yourself as having conquered the day even before you start gives you the upper hand on facing what's coming. Below is an example of things you can do to set up a positive morning routine centered around visualization.

The steps	Optional activities	Recommended duration	The benefits
Silence	Breath exercises, journaling, luxury reading, meditation, yoga, and so on	About 5 minutes	Improves focus, self-awareness, relaxation, and serenity for the day ahead
Exercise	Sports, running, Pilates, gym, swimming, and so on	20–25 minutes	Increases energy, emotional well-being, excitement, and vitality
Visualization	Guided imagery, harnessing positive thinking through affirmations, envisioning the successes of the day ahead, and so on	5–10 minutes	Promotes calmness, confidence, eagerness, and success

Going into silence mode as soon as you wake up allows you to make the most of your fresh morning mind before the day's responsibilities start influencing it. You gain control over your thoughts as you bring positivity and gratitude into your morning silence. Having quiet time first thing in the morning is far better than reaching for things that stress you out, such as emails, your work diary, or responsibilities. You set the tone for the day by starting with your peace. Then, more into exercising to get the blood flowing and the body engaged. Followed by visualization after a nice hot shower. Of course, you can always swap the exercise and visualization components to do what works best for you.

Visualization Breaks During the Day

Unlike the mornings, you have less time during breaks to have a full-on visualization routine. So, optimal use of your time is key. Taking short, scheduled breaks for quick visualization exercises throughout the day can reinforce personal goals. Take five minutes to affirm yourself and remember the foundation you laid for yourself in the morning. Visualization during breaks helps maintain a positive mindset when feeling daily stresses.

Opt for a quick stroll outside and stand in the sun with headphones playing your favorite song. You can also grab lunch outside with a group of colleagues whose company you enjoy. Have positive break-time conversations that reinforce your goals for the day.

Evening Reflection Through Visualization

Use visualization in the evening to reflect on the day's achievements. Go back home after work and spend some time visualizing. Similar to your morning schedule, appreciate what you achieved during the day while planning for the future. View your evening reflection as an opportunity to visualize the next steps, fostering a positive outlook and readiness for the following day.

Role of Visualization in Problem-Solving

Visualizing different outcomes and approaches can help with complex problem-solving and decision-making. Through visualization, you prepare your mind for what you want and the work it takes to achieve it. Harnessing the benefits of visualization, such as relaxation, motivation, imagination, and mental clarity, gives you a positive edge when it comes to problem-solving. Visualization can help you navigate daily complexities and make informed decisions during stressful periods.

Visualizing Outcomes to Enhance Decision-Making

Using visualization effectively involves taking logical steps to realize your goals. In the process of doing so, you can also take constructive feedback and view setbacks as opportunities as you continue to achieve what you set out. Visualizing potential outcomes can help you foresee possible issues and assess solutions beforehand. Therefore, this reduces uncertainty and enhances decision-making confidence. Since visualization puts what you want into focus, you are more likely to make decisions based on that guidance, making you a more decisive person overall.

Creative Problem Solving with Visualization

Creative problem-solving begins with visualization. You need to identify and envision your desired outcome. Knowing what you want is a crucial first step to achieving it. This way, when you are faced with problems, you can implement solutions that keep your goal in mind. Once you know your goal and you've identified problems that get in the way of it, you creatively problem-solve by highlighting valuable solutions that you can use to overcome these barriers.

Visualization also unlocks creative problem-solving by allowing you to explore different scenarios mentally. It inspires innovative solutions that might not be apparent initially but benefit future outcomes.

Strategic Visualization in Professional Settings

Visualization helps you take action toward your goals, no matter the context. Fortunately, the same visualization techniques that enhance your personal experiences can also improve your professional life. Using strategic visualization in business or professional settings helps you anticipate challenges and envision yourself successfully navigating complex projects or negotiations.

You can enter group settings with a positive mindset, fully determined to reach a common outcome.

Strategic visualization at work provides direction to help you and your co-workers decide where to put your energy. It also helps you avoid unproductive work conflict while maximizing your resources and opportunities. Strategic visualization helps the team highlight the company's long- and short-term goals, rooted in specific, achievable, relevant, and time-bound goals.

Through active listening, positivity, collaboration, and visualization, you and your team can come up with shared solutions to work-related issues. Strategic visualization in professional settings is great for reinforcing a proactive and positive approach.

Whether in a personal or professional setting, visualization is proof that you truly do become what you think! So, where you put your focus in the form of what you choose to think about can really influence your mental health. The next chapter explores positive thinking and its impact on mental well-being.

Chapter 9:
Maintaining Your Mental Health

Positive thinking has benefits for mental health. Maintaining good mental health isn't about being happy all the time but about finding healthy ways to cope with life's obstacles and constantly being aware of your needs at any given time. Your mental well-being influences every aspect of your life. If you aren't taking care of how you feel, what you need, your boundaries, and so on, then your mental well-being is threatened.

Maintaining mental well-being is possible, even when you have been diagnosed with a mental health condition. It's all about taking care of yourself and approaching life positively. Taking care of your mental well-being has many physical benefits, including lower blood pressure, stress reduction, illness prevention, and greater pain tolerance. The advantages don't stop there because mental health also benefits your mood, creativity, cognitive functions, and skills. You learn how to cope with situations constructively and find healthy ways to problem-solve. Mental well-being allows you to think clearly as well, making it possible to face challenges with a cool head.

Since mental well-being is essential to how you approach life, it's helpful to gain more insight into the topic. This chapter discusses the vital role of continuous positive thinking in maintaining mental health and preventing burnout.

Identifying Stressors and Triggers

The bills are due, your family needs you, and work keeps piling up; these are just some examples of how stressful life can be. Having work and getting to care for the family is a blessing, but sometimes, naturally, it overwhelms even the best of us. You aren't alone in experiencing life's stressors. However, your mental health only benefits when you identify what these are and positively work through them.

Stress is your body's response to responsibilities and the world's pressures. Sources of stress, also known as stressors, are triggers that can be internal or external. Stress can be short-term or over a more extended period, and all experiences can feel overwhelming. They can have a toiling effect on mental well-being.

Recognizing what your stressors are is the first step in managing them. By identifying your triggers, whether it's relationships, life changes, or unpredictable events, you've taken the leap toward solving the problem. Learning to manage your stress is beneficial for mental health. Though stress is a natural part of life, it shouldn't consume you. You need to find ways to process it so you can gracefully handle what life throws at you.

Personal Reflection and Journaling

You can start identifying your stressors through journaling and personal reflection. These tools allow you to explore your thoughts, fears, and some of the internal stressors that keep you in a stress cycle. Once you've identified these, you allow yourself to ease your stress.

Take 10–15 minutes to write down your feelings and explore your stress-related thoughts. Once you have your feelings and stressors on paper, positively reflect on solutions that can help you navigate this stress daily. If you are unsure how to start your personal reflection and journaling, consider the following prompts.

- What are you feeling today? (Name the feeling or list the combination of feelings if you are experiencing a mixture of emotions).

- What are some of the things that have caused you to feel this way? (Explore the stressors that got you to this point, no matter how small they might seem).

- What was your biggest challenge today?

- Where do you feel stress in your body?

- What are small, manageable steps you can take to reduce stress?

- How can you reframe stress to see the situation from a more constructive perspective?

- How can you show up for yourself to help ease your stress? (Think of ideas for self-care at this moment because you need it).

- Who can you reach out to for support?

- What are some positive things you can say to yourself about this moment? (It's important to avoid focusing only on the unpleasant things about your day).

- How can you plan better for tomorrow to avoid the same stress trigger?

- How will you respond better if the same trigger occurs?

How you approach your journaling is purely up to you. It's essential to do what you feel most comfortable with and what flows. You can write your reflections in paragraphs or opt for bullet journaling. It doesn't matter how you go about it, so long as you permit yourself to spend some time in quietude, decluttering your headspace. You can even share your insights with your therapist or a trusted friend who can help you reflect further on what you've written.

Personal reflection and journaling can help you track daily experiences and identify patterns that lead to stress. It's important to acknowledge your stressors and emotions without judging them. The aim of personal reflection isn't to self-condemn or shame but to overcome the challenges you sometimes face. Expressing your thoughts and sorting through feelings contribute to a better mental state. You can use your discoveries to foster a proactive approach to managing stressors with a positive mindset.

Mindfulness and Awareness Training

Mindfulness involves bringing awareness to the situation in a nonjudgmental way. So, your personal reactions are an example of both mindfulness and awareness in action. Mindfulness and increased awareness help you recognize the onset of stress and triggers in real-time. This allows you to apply immediate positive interventions to maintain mental equilibrium. Practices like yoga, breathwork, and meditation are all great for achieving mindfulness and awareness.

You can practice mindfulness and awareness at any time of the day and anywhere. Using your mind as a resource for a positive perspective promotes mindfulness in your life. For example, if you are on break, you can be mindful by being attentive to your experience. Observe how your food tastes as you eat it; notice the colors, smells, and textures. Being fully present as you eat your lunch during a break is a form of mindfulness and awareness. When you focus on the moment, the good in the current situation, and what you are learning now, you won't have time to drift to the future or past, finding things that make you anxious.

Environmental Adjustments

Changing your environment can minimize exposure to known stressors because positive changes can enhance mental wellness. Your home, workplace, and environment will reduce or contribute to stress. Factors such as noise, pollution, darker areas, overcrowding, and lack of privacy can cause irritability and anxiety. However, calmer areas, with natural light, bright colors, soft textures, and quiet, can inspire feelings of peace, having a positive influence on mental health.

Natural settings are also optimal for mental health. Parks, beaches, other bodies of water, and forests positively influence your mental well-being. Studies show natural environments boost cognitive function, improve mood, and ease stress. Taking walks in nature can be restorative, allowing you to connect to the natural beauty of life.

Understanding the connection between your environment and mental health is essential to maintaining positivity. Being in environments that promote mental health, positive thinking, and calmness is beneficial.

Role of Physical Activity in Mental Health

Exercise benefits your body—you know that already—but it's also hugely beneficial for your mind. Physical activity can improve sleep and emotional states and help you manage stress better. Running, cycling, and walking are all examples of physical activities that can improve mental health.

Exercise as a Natural Antidepressant

Studies have found that physical activity can act as an antidepressant, making mild to moderate depression more manageable (Robinson et al., 2024). Getting physically active is also known to relieve symptoms of major depression and sometimes ease its intensity by 26% (Robinson et al., 2024). Physical activity releases endorphins and other natural brain chemicals that can enhance feelings of well-being, meaning you can use exercise to cultivate a positive mood.

When you exercise, it relieves tension from your body and stress from your mind. Exercising enhances your mental and physical health by boosting your energy and focus. Anything that promotes movement can help you be more productive and attentive throughout the day. A simple walk on the beach or a hike up mountain trails can refresh the mind, promote quality sleep, and sharpen memory.

Exercise is a natural antidepressant that promotes cognitive development and brain health and reduces inflammation. Your body and mind feel energized and good after a physical activity session. Exercise also enables you to think more clearly and positively so you can make helpful decisions that benefit your life.

Routine Integration

Regular exercise can help you get the most out of your workout. Exercising isn't a once-off practice; it needs to be prioritized daily or at least a couple of days a week. Integrating physical activity into daily routines, regardless of lifestyle, ensures consistent benefits. A small daily investment in physical health can yield significant positive mental health returns.

Physical activity doesn't have to feel forced or like a monotonous chore. Instead, you can make it a part of daily fun. Incorporate exercise into your routine through recreational activities. For example, if you live in a safe neighborhood with convenience stores nearby, it can be helpful to walk or cycle to places rather than drive. You can make exercise fun and unstructured by carving out time for play. Go outside and skip rope with your family, engage in tug-of-war with trusted friends, or play volleyball with fellow beach lovers. Exercise can be all about enjoying yourself with loved ones while getting a good sweat.

Sports are also a great physical outlet. They are a more structured form of exercise where you can play tennis, basketball, rowing, and any other enjoyable sport you can think of. Your daily physical activity is your choice, and deciding on something you'll want to do every day is advantageous. Activities you enjoy are more easily integrated into your daily routine.

Social Sports and Group Fitness

Competitive activities such as sports and group fitness can motivate you to stay on track with your fitness. Football, baseball, athletics, CrossFit, and Zumba classes are all examples of activities you can take on. Combining exercise and social interaction can give you the mental health boost you need. You get to share your time with supportive people who enjoy the same activities you do. Also, social sports and group fitness are ways of collaborating on a common goal with people, which is known to have positive mental health effects.

Nutrition and Mental Well-Being

What you put into your body impacts your mental health, just as how often you exercise. Good nutrition promotes neural development, physical health, and mental well-being. Eating healthy can help you cope with daily stressors, maintain energy, and stay focused throughout the day. People who eat well have a balanced nutritional diet associated with positive mental health outcomes.

Brain Foods for Positive Thinking

Nutritional psychiatry focuses on the connection between the brain and gut, known as the food-and-mood or diet-brain association (Blain, 2022). It ultimately highlights how food influences mood and neural functioning. High-quality foods containing antioxidants, minerals, and vitamins nourish the brain, helping it function optimally.

What you eat has disease prevention and healing power. Specific foods such as omega-3 fatty acids, whole grains, and leafy greens enhance cognitive function and improve mood. Healthy dietary choices support a positive mindset. Let's explore some feel-good dietary options that you can include in your shopping cart.

Veggies and Fruit

With the natural sugars and fibers offered by fruits and vegetables, these are great supplements for your well-being. The nourishment you get from veggies and fruits optimizes brain health and contributes to healthy cognitive and emotional regulation. Below is a list of items you might want to consider.

Fruits

- blackberries

- black currants

- blueberries

- figs

- plums

- prunes

Vegetables

- beets

- purple yam

- eggplant

- purple cabbage

- carrots

- radishes

Nuts

With added nutritional benefits, nuts should be at the top of your list. Nuts have antiaging properties, brain-boosting nutrients, and immune protectors. A variety of nuts makes for a good snack between meals, improving heart health, autoimmune functioning, and neural wellness. Below is a list of the ones you should keep in mind.

- walnuts

- sunflower seeds

- almonds

- pine nuts

- macadamia

- cashew

- hazelnuts

Seafood

Eating seafood transfers essential nutrients to support cognitive well-being. Most seafood is omega-3 fatty acids and protein. Studies confirm that eating seafood boosts your body with vitamins D, E, B12, and A, as well as iodine and fatty acids. Below is a list of options to choose from.

- fish

- prawns

- crab

- mussels

- salmon

Lean Meats and Poultry

Everything in moderation is a great philosophy. You can have some lean meat (lower salts and fats) in your diet, and poultry is also a great addition.

Lean meats

- beef

- lamb chops

- veal

- pork

Poultry

- duck

- chicken

- turkey

Legumes or Beans

You can also get nutrients from beans, which are essential in vegan and vegetarian communities. Including these as part of your diet is beneficial. Below are a few examples of legumes.

- all beans

- lentils

- chickpeas

- split peas

Healthy food can be a source of iron, zinc, and vitamin C. Eating healthy is all about balance. You can feel sluggish if you eat too many "feel-good" foods and neglect the variety on your plate. It's essential to balance your veggies and fruits with stable foods. Finding a good range of foods to include in your diet will leave you feeling upbeat, productive, and ready to tackle each day.

Impact of Hydration on Cognitive Function

The role of hydration in cognitive function is often overlooked. Nutritionists suggest six to eight glasses of water daily (Nicholls, 2024). Talking to a nutritionist about your water and diet can be beneficial to ensure you meet your needs. Staying hydrated promotes mood stability, cell rejuvenation, and mental clarity. Water intake is a simple but effective strategy for maintaining mental clarity and positivity.

Meal Planning for Mental Health

Sometimes, deciding what to eat every day can be stressful. When you come back from work, the last thing you want to be thinking about is what you are going to put on a plate; unless you find the cooking and impromptu planning fun. However, for those of us who prefer to preplan meals, the following information can be helpful.

When people feel overwhelmed about what to eat, they're more likely to do the easy thing and get takeout. Yet, when you preplan your meals, you can relax for the week, knowing you have food waiting for you. Planning meals that balance blood sugar levels throughout the day can prevent mood swings and contribute to a stable, positive outlook.

Your meal plan and preparation are up to you. As long as your fridge is filled with quality options, you can quickly prepare stress-free meals. Below is an example of how you can structure your meal plan from the first to the seventh day of the week.

Monday

Breakfast	Oatmeal and blueberries
Lunch	Turkey and avocado lettuce wrap
Snack	Mixed unsalted nuts
Dinner	Salmon with broccoli and a type of grain (wheat or rice)
Dessert (Optional)	A square of dark chocolate

Tuesday

Breakfast	Two boiled eggs on whole-grain toast
Lunch	Tuna roll with brown rice
Snack	Carrot sticks and hummus
Dinner	Grilled chicken with barley and spinach
Dessert (Optional)	Melon with plain nonfat yogurt (Greek yogurt)

Wednesday	
Breakfast	
Lunch	
Snack	
Dinner	
Dessert (Optional)	

Thursday	
Breakfast	
Lunch	
Snack	
Dinner	
Dessert (Optional)	

Friday	
Breakfast	
Lunch	
Snack	
Dinner	
Dessert (Optional)	

Saturday	
Breakfast	
Lunch	
Snack	
Dinner	
Dessert (Optional)	

Sunday	
Breakfast	
Lunch	
Snack	
Dinner	
Dessert (Optional)	

The first two examples are to guide a personal dietary plan that can keep you focused on healthy eating. Remember to have water between meals or even with meals. A great hydration plan is to have two glasses before every meal. So drink two full glasses before breakfast, another before lunch, and another before dinner. During your snack time, you can have one glass before and another after the snack. Weekends can be used for grocery shopping and planning food for the upcoming week.

Sleep's Impact on Mental Health

Your diet plays a role in the quality of sleep you get, and sleep influences mental health. Imagine a time when you were running low on sleep. Do you remember how cranky you were? Sleep deprivation often means a lack of energy, so you don't have the fuel to be productive, cooperative, friendly, and fun. When you schedule and prioritize sleep, you prevent brain fog, mood irregularities, impulsivity, and psychological strain.

However, getting enough sleep facilitates positive neural functioning, helping your brain process emotions and experiences more effectively. During your sleep cycle, the mind is given an opportunity to rest and reboot. Memories, thoughts, and associations are cemented as you sleep, preventing mental decline and improving energy.

Sleep Hygiene Practices

Poor sleep habits are typically associated with poor sleep hygiene practices. Improving your sleep hygiene habits can increase your quality of sleep. Sleep hygiene practices reduce interruptions and promote peaceful nights. Some examples of good sleep hygiene include having a consistent bedtime, creating a routine, and winding down before bed. Sleeping at the same time every night helps your mind build the habit, allowing you to get sufficient rest.

Winding down before bed looks like leaving your electronic devices on the side table and not touching them for at least an hour before bed. Phone screens and bright lights can prevent falling asleep, so putting those items away prepares your brain for rest.

Brushing your teeth, washing your face or showering, and getting into warm pajamas are also great bedtime routines. Dim the lights in your home and avoid caffeine before bed; all of these tips are good sleep hygiene practices. Optimize your sleep environment to encourage restorative sleep. It's essential for positive thinking and mental health.

Link Between Sleep and Emotional Regulation

Adequate sleep helps with emotional regulation and resilience, which are crucial for maintaining a positive outlook in the face of daily stresses. Emotional reactivity is less frequent with good sleep. You become better at processing stressful experiences and regulating how you respond to them. Sleep makes you a more calm, responsive, and solution-driven person.

Technological Impacts on Sleep

Blue light from screens negatively impacts the quality of your sleep because the brightness suppresses melatonin production—otherwise known as the sleep hormone (Alshoaibi et al., 2023). This makes it hard for your brain to rest at night, increasing the chances of sleep irregularities. However, implementing positive sleep hygiene practices can help avoid the negative impacts of technology on sleep. Positive habits like limiting screen time before bed enhance sleep quality and, by extension, mental health.

Making positive adjustments to your life, no matter how small they might seem, is an essential step toward living a positively transformed life. The next chapter explores what transformation can be for you when you practice positive thinking and helpful habits daily.

Chapter 10:
Living a Positively Transformed Life

Positive thinking begins by altering your thoughts and perspective, thereby transforming your life. Vision boards, affirmations, and manifestations are all associated with the desire to grow and evolve for the better. Living positively transformed requires a shift in your actions, which begins with a positive shift in your mind. A life of fulfillment comes from learning to master resilience, regulate emotions, and have a positive outlook on obstacles.

Positive thinking is a lifestyle decision that leads to personal growth and enhances mental health. People who focus on positive outcomes and solutions rather than sinking into a spiral of negative thoughts tend to live more optimistically. This brings joy and cultivates connection in their lives. You can be one of those people. If you allow yourself to reframe negativity into positive thinking, you'll also cultivate connections, enhance mental health, and experience deep joy. It's all about deciding to be a positive thinker and then actively working toward it.

Remember, positive thinking doesn't happen overnight. For many, it's a journey of commitment, reflection, and continuous choices. Personal transformation is rooted in positive thinking practices, and Chapters 2, 3, 7, and 8 are key indicators of how. Feel free to go back to those chapters and reflect on them to form the foundation for this chapter. This chapter is about stepping into a life transformed by positivity, where everyday challenges are met with optimism and seen as opportunities for transformation.

Sustaining Positivity in Daily Life

Your thoughts manifest your reality. If you have stressful, negative thoughts, you are more likely to experience life that way, too. Sustaining positivity in daily life is actually about actively creating your reality by implementing positive strategies, such as affirmations, self-assessment, realistic expectations, and adaptation. Let's dive into these.

Routine Positive Affirmations

Vocalizing positive intentions through affirmations can help you transform your personal and professional ambitions into a lived reality. It's scientific! Through neuroplasticity, positive affirmations eventually create new neural pathways (Perry, 2024b). Your association with positivity and affirmations might be weak at first. You might even feel a sense of discomfort after saying a few positive statements, but keep going. Over time, the old, negative neural pathways will change to reflect the newer, more positive ones.

Positive affirmations should be centered around your values and personal goals to provide a clear direction toward positive outcomes. Using affirmations to reinforce positivity enhances self-esteem and helps you maintain a positive mindset daily.

You can write down some affirmations on sticky notes and plaster them somewhere visible. Some examples of affirmations that can positively transform your life are listed below.

- I can learn any skill if I give myself time.

- I can do difficult things.

- I am constantly learning.

- I am resilient enough to overcome challenges.

- Doing my best is enough.

- I am allowed to prioritize my health.

- I view my experiences and emotions nonjudgmentally.

- I am safe, capable, and supported.

Repetition is key to creating a routine of positive affirmations. When you continuously affirm yourself and your situation, you embed positive phrases into your subconscious. Repetition makes it possible to transform default negative thoughts into more positive patterns of thinking and behaving.

Positive affirmations are a step toward taking charge of your life. Reflecting on affirmations daily is essential to allow the message to translate into your experiences.

Affirmations bring meaningfulness into life by filling experiences with positivity. The words you repeat over yourself daily might seem simple, but they slowly change how your mind processes experiences.

What you think truly is who you become because if you relate something long enough, it eventually translates as truth. That's why we often think something and automatically take it as fact. Thoughts are genuinely powerful. So your positive affirmations might start as something you don't believe in, but through repetition, it will automate your default thinking pattern.

Positive Interaction Rituals

Establishing rituals that foster positive interactions, such as starting each day by sharing a positive thought with a loved one or team, can set a constructive tone for the day. Positive interactions are integral to sustaining positivity in life. The same way you affirm yourself every day, or should anyway, is how you can enhance positive interaction with others. Make sure to compliment people when you see them doing something good. Also, offer constructive feedback to loved ones when requested.

Positive interaction rituals are all about spreading positivity around with the people in your life. So listen attentively, show interest by asking questions, call someone randomly to remind them that you love them, and so on.

Mindset Resets

Techniques for quick mental resets, such as focused breathing or a short walk, can help restore a positive outlook when facing daily stressors. The habit of mindset resets is instilled over time. You need to first get into the habit of taking care of yourself through rest, positive self-talk, taking breaks, and being grateful. When these experiences are ingrained in your behavior, resetting your mindset to attract positivity in situations becomes more accessible.

Reflective Practices for Self-Assessment

Reflection allows you to process emotions, assess your progress, make positive connections, and develop self-awareness and meaning. Practicing self-assessment can help you embrace positivity and sustain it in your life because it shows you what works and what might need improving. Techniques that you can use to facilitate personal reflection include structured journaling, meditative reflection, and feedback loops.

Structured Journaling Techniques

Structured journaling methods, like gratitude journaling or the "three good things" exercise, can help individuals focus on positive aspects of their lives and reinforce a positive mindset. Making time for self-assessment is essential. It can help you navigate life's obstacles mindfully and with compassion. Reflective journaling is therapeutic; it empowers you and gives your mind a breakthrough in self-expression. Embracing structured journaling helps you explore complex emotions and situations to reach awakening and mental clarity. You can unlock ease, positivity, and calmness with structured journaling techniques.

Gratitude Journaling

Commit at least five minutes daily to reflect on what you are grateful for. In this reflection, you can write down about five things. Gratitude is profound sustenance for positivity. It turns you away from the negative situations you might be experiencing and helps you see the bright side of your experiences. Gratitude journaling can shift your mindset from self-pity to empowerment.

Instead of focusing on life's problems, you can focus on solutions and the abundance that already exists. Gratitude helps you appreciate what you have, improving your mental health, perspective, and optimism. When you journal what you are grateful for, the brain has no choice but to become more sensitive to the good things in life, fostering a sense of fulfillment and sustained positivity.

Self-Compassion Journaling

Sometimes, we can be our greatest enemies. Our minds can convince us of negative things about ourselves that might not even be true. Self-compassion journaling is a way to curb these cognitive distortions. Consider writing a letter of compassion to yourself. Think of the task as though you are communicating with a friend.

Too often, we struggle to see ourselves from a friendship perspective, and self-compassion journaling can help with that. In the journal, make a note about your self-image and a mistake you are battling to forgive yourself for. Then, in the letter, show yourself compassion. Understand and accept your mistakes and be kind.

Once you've highlighted what you need to forgive, draft a letter to yourself. Outline your strengths, offer yourself some encouraging words, and forgive. Self-compassion journaling can help you change negative self-talk to a more positive aspect. It promotes compassion and a healthier connection with yourself, which is necessary for bonding with others.

Unfiltered Journaling

Set a timer and allow yourself to write your thoughts without interruption or pause. Unfiltered journaling is about letting your thoughts flow without worrying about grammar, comprehension, and spelling. Allow yourself to declutter your mind space. Journaling in this way helps you bypass the innate tendency to judge and change your thoughts, allowing you to gain deeper self-awareness. You get to process your emotional experiences and solve problems more creatively. Unfiltered journaling encourages self-discovery, leading to sustained positivity, enlightenment, and breakthroughs.

Meditative Reflection

All mediation allows you to be patient, present, and purposeful from moment to moment. Meditative reflection involves sitting with yourself and truly embracing what you feel and why you are. When you practice meditative reflection, it helps you become more aware of your cognitive state. It's about intentionally spending time away from distractions to welcome stillness comfortably.

Use gentle breathing to usher awareness into a moment. Pay attention to your physical sensations, the sounds around you, and emotions as they arise. Let your thoughts pass through your mind without trying to force them to be something else. You can do this for 10 to 15 minutes daily.

Regular meditation calms the mind and provides clarity, allowing individuals to reflect on their thoughts and feelings from a place of grounded positivity. Meditative reflection is beneficial because it allows you to organize your priorities and identify your strengths. Meditative reflection helps you reevaluate your principles and values in a nonjudgmental manner.

Feedback Loops with Trusted Peers

Regular feedback sessions with trusted friends or mentors can offer you an external perspective on personal growth and areas for improvement. Feedback loops can motivate you to learn more about yourself. When you permit and receive feedback from your trusted peers, you learn how your environment responds to your strengths, weaknesses, and talents. It gives you ample opportunities to be held accountable for your behaviors, helping you become more responsible. Through feedback, you also get the chance to build genuine connections by seeing yourself from another person's perspective.

Creating positive feedback loops encourages continuous transformation. Trusted peers can strengthen your communication skills. You can develop your ability to talk directly to people, ask relevant questions, foster mutual understanding, get help, and regularly learn new things about yourself.

Balancing Positivity with Realistic Expectations

Positive thinking can push you forward, but unchecked positivity leads to unrealistic expectations. It's essential to find a balance between positivity and realism. Being realistic offers a clear understanding of the actions that will follow your positivity. For example, if you positively believe that you will get a promotion, you realistically should be developing your skills in preparation for that opportunity. You know that positivity and realistic expectations are balanced when you can act on what you hope for.

Setting Achievable Goals

Positive action isn't possible without achievable goals. Setting realistic and attainable goals is crucial because it can prevent frustration and maintain motivation, thereby supporting a sustained positive outlook. Your goals should encompass your vision for the future. Setting goals takes thoughtfulness; it's about highlighting what you want to achieve. A goal is achievable when small steps are outlined to help you achieve the bigger picture.

Your goals should be internally motivated by what you enjoy and the principles you uphold. Setting achievable goals won't help if the intention is based on external motivations. So you need to know your values and let those motivate you. Consider what inspires you and what you're passionate about. Setting goals guided by what's meaningful to you will give you a sense of determination to accomplish them.

Also, setting achievable goals involves taking time to visualize future outcomes. This is where your vision board comes in. Based on your goals, lay out what your ideal future will entail. Consider what resources you need to achieve your goals and how you'll get them.

Tip For Setting Goals

To help you set robust and achievable goals, you can use the acronym "SMART." This stands for setting specific, measurable, achievable, relevant, and time-bound goals (Perry, 2022a).

- Specific: Your goals should focus on particular areas of improvement. For example, "I want to improve my fitness."

- Measurable: Goals should also align with certain metrics to help you make them actionable. For example, "I'll set up appointments for three days a week with my trainer."

- Achievable: Your goals must be realistically based on expectations you can achieve with practice. For example, "Going to my appointments every three days."

- Relevant: Goals should complement your values, ambitions, and hopes so you can continuously move in a positive direction.

- Time-bound: Your goals should be based on a specific timeframe. So create a deadline for yourself for when to evaluate your progress and when you want the goal to be achieved.

Achievable goals are also those that you can control. Your goals should enable you to progress. So set tasks for yourself of things that you can do. Goals shouldn't depend on others or rely on factors outside of your control. This means being realistic and accountable to the goals you have for yourself.

Embracing Constructive Criticism

Constructive criticism can be viewed positively as a tool for growth and improvement rather than a setback, integrating it into a realistic yet optimistic life approach. When you receive constructive criticism, learn to nod and accept what's being said. Consider how you can use the feedback to improve yourself rather than feel insulted.

Try not to get defensive. Of course, it can be hard to listen to criticism, even when it's constructive. However, you will be open to opposing views if you are committed to your transformation. Take a few deep breaths during the conversation to truly process what's being communicated. Embracing constructive criticism helps you be respectful toward the person giving the feedback and learn from it. Remember, embracing constructive criticism from people who want the best for you will help you improve in how you welcome it.

Awareness of Cognitive Biases

Cognitive biases will significantly affect your choices and actions moving forward. Understanding how certain biases affect your thinking can help you approach them positively. Awareness is crucial in recognizing and adjusting for natural cognitive biases, such as optimism bias, which can skew the perception of reality and lead to disappointments. Consider the common distortions from Chapter 3; when you are aware of your own, it will help you sustain positivity.

Adapting Positivity to Changing Life Stages

Positive thinking can help you adapt to adversity and life stages as things change. Life's unpredictability requires adjustment, adaptation, and resilience, all of which come from having a positive attitude. Adapting positively to life's stages involves changing your perspective, feelings, and behaviors to cope with complex, unexpected, or difficult situations. You should be open to change and embrace changes as growth opportunities.

Although inevitable, change can cause anxiety because of the uncertainty that comes with it. However, adapting to it with a positive attitude can help you manage the strong emotions that come with the uncertainty. Adapting positivity to changing life stages involves embracing what comes, which reduces stress and improves confidence in your ability to cope with the unknown.

Adapting positivity to changing life stages is beneficial professionally and personally; it can help you learn continuously. Positively adapting requires acceptance, awareness, and learning. It's all about recognizing when changes happen and accepting that these are inevitable and helpful. Changing life stages occur, and positivity can help you handle them confidently.

Age-Specific Positive Thinking Techniques

Embracing change is essential to coping positively with life's transitions, regardless of your age. Daily routines, relationships, jobs, and personal goals are susceptible to change. So positive thinking can help you manage these as they come and make the best of each stage of life.

Flexibility is a positive thinking technique that helps young people transition from school to the work environment and older people from work to retirement. It's essential to be flexible with life's experiences so you can pivot in situations that require it. Also, recognizing your fears about change will help you normalize this emotion and prevent you from resisting it.

Rather than dwell in the scariness of what you don't know yet, embrace the endless possibilities that come with life's changes. Shift your mindset to acknowledge the opportunities that come with embracing the uncertainty. When you don't treat life's changes as something forced on you but instead embrace them as an active choice, you end up feeling empowered. Embracing change at any age reframes it more positively.

Positive thinking techniques can be adapted for different life stages. For instance, older adults might focus on positivity through legacy-building activities, while younger people might focus on career and personal development. Focusing your energy into creating something purposeful can help you adapt positivity to life changes.

Anticipating Life Transitions

Anticipating and positively managing life transitions, such as moving to a new city, changing careers, or entering retirement, takes time. If you keep positivity in mind during transitions, you can use changes as growth opportunities. Any kind of change shapes how you view yourself, your relationships, and the role you are supposed to play in different transitions.

Life's transitions vary. The types that you anticipate are usually expected to happen as part of a natural progression. For example, getting a job in your adult life is a transition that you can anticipate, together with choosing to study further, get married, or move homes.

However, not all transitions can be anticipated. Sometimes, changes are completely out of the blue or unexpected. Unanticipated transitions are those you couldn't plan for, even if you did your best to be prepared. For example, illness, accidents, loss, or relationship breakdowns. These are usually hurtful challenges that require emotional regulation to overcome them. This doesn't mean unanticipated transitions are all negative. For instance, a sudden job promotion can be a positive transition that you might not be prepared for. Also, an unexpected pregnancy can be a welcomed surprise for many families.

Regardless of your stage, it's essential to be patient during your transitions. Change demands curiosity and constant self-compassion for you to thrive in it.

Lifelong Learning as a Tool for Adaptation

Lifelong learning plays a significant role in helping you adapt to life's transitions. When you expand your curiosity and approach changes with eagerness to learn, you maintain a positive outlook that keeps your mind engaged and optimistic. Lifelong learning helps you continually adapt to new information and experiences.

Equally, lifelong learning is a secret weapon for self-awareness. You discover things about yourself that you might not have realized if you weren't eager to keep learning. Committing to lifelong learning can help you form genuine connections with people, be resilient in the face of setbacks—because you see them in a positive light—and adapt to challenging situations. Lifelong learning is a tool for adaptation because it empowers you with the perspective that every experience is a chance to gain new information. As such, you view obstacles as opportunities to acquire knowledge and continue to grow.

Strategies for lifelong learning are listed below:

- setting clear goals

- finding different learning resources (online, in-person, organizations, and MasterClasses)

- listening when others speak

- developing a positive mindset toward challenges

- reflection

- social connection

The principle that education doesn't just happen at school is at the center of lifelong learning. When you embrace continuous learning as a tool for adaptation, you allow yourself to develop interpersonal skills, self-awareness, and coping mechanisms. Activities such as workshops, joining classes, and absorbing new competencies encourage positive thinking. Lifelong learning allows you to pursue new hobbies and develop skills, which leads to fulfillment and purpose in life.

Interpersonal skills develop when you realize that other people are valuable because they have something unique to offer. Everyone you meet can teach you something, and recognizing that truth helps you achieve lifelong learning. You stay open to what others have to share and thus continue to adopt new perspectives and knowledge. In today's busy and ever-changing world, positive thinking can lead to collaborative efforts, personal growth, and overall success through lifelong learning.

Conclusion

Curve balls and unpredictable events are a part of life, and positive thinking can help you manage them. The quality of your thoughts influences the experiences that you encounter in your life. The more you embrace positive thinking, the more positivism you'll begin to experience in your lifetime. Positivity doesn't take away life's challenges but changes how you approach them. As a positive thinker, you become more equipped to confront obstacles because your mindset toward them is one of confidence and transformation.

Harnessing the power of positive thinking requires effort, mindfulness, gratitude, and willingness to grow. Perceiving experiences positively yields immense rewards for yourself, your relationships, and your performance. You begin to soar to new heights, cherishing friendships and other connections, building resilience, and increasing mindfulness.

Positive thinking demands you to reframe negative beliefs about yourself and the world around you. It's about viewing situations through a constructive lens, whereby challenges become opportunities and successes are celebrations. Letting yourself be open to endless possibilities and outcomes will enrich your life. Positivity helps you attract what you want to experience. If something unpleasant happens, your positive mindset allows you to embrace it as a positive. Your positivity offers a clear picture of your experiences so you can create constructive plans, set clear goals, and act accordingly.

Although you might occasionally find some situations frustrating—and that's okay—positivity enhances those situations by shifting your attention toward what you can learn and use to move forward. This also makes it possible to contribute positively to other people's experiences.

When you permit yourself to develop positive thinking habits, you promote health, success, joy, and comprehensive problem-solving. Through positive thinking, you learn to focus on what you want and create ways to obtain it. Of course, positive thinking is a practice that takes practice and repetition to change negative thinking patterns. Affirmations, vision boards, social connections, positive feedback, and wholesome interactions are among many things that promote positivity.

Like any skill, positive thinking requires consistent effort to master, so feel encouraged to keep applying the techniques you've learned. Take what you've learned from this book and make positive changes in your life and the lives of others. Spread positivity and actively create the habits you want to see manifest in your life.

References

Ackerman, C. E. (2018, July 5). *Positive mindset: how to develop a positive mental attitude.* Positive Psychology. https://positivepsychology.com/positive-mindset/

Ackerman, C. E. (2018, April 20). *What is positive psychology & why is it important?* Positive Psychology. https://positivepsychology.com/what-is-positive-psychology-definition/

Aging gracefully: the power of positive thinking. (n.d.). Senior Friendship Centers. https://friendshipcenters.org/aging-gracefully-the-power-of-positive-thinking/

Allen, S. (2019, February). *Positive neuroscience.* Greater Good Science Center. https://ggsc.berkeley.edu/images/uploads/White_Paper_Positive_Neuroscience_FINAL.pdf

Alshoaibi, Y., Bafil, W., & Rahim, M. (2023). The effect of screen use on sleep quality among adolescents in Riyadh, Saudi Arabia. *Journal of Family Medicine*

and Primary Care, 12(7), 1379-1388.
https://doi.org/10.4103/jfmpc.jfmpc_159_23

The anatomy of a habit: Cue, routine, and reward. (n.d.). Kinnu.
https://kinnu.xyz/kinnuverse/lifestyle/healthy-
habits/the-anatomy-of-a-habit-cue-routine-and-
reward/

Andreev, I. (2021, December 19). *Constructive feedback.*
Valamis.
https://www.valamis.com/hub/constructive-
feedback

Andruşca, A. (2023, August 16). *Neural pathways.*
KenHub.
https://www.kenhub.com/en/library/anatomy
/neural-pathways

Ascent Global Partners. (2023, December 20). *Balancing
optimism and realism: setting realistic expectations in
your job search.* LinkedIn.
https://www.linkedin.com/pulse/balancing-
optimism-realism-setting-realistic-expectations-
rav9c

Atta, S. (2023, August 16). *How changing your thought
patterns can transform your perspective and boost your*

mood.   Medium.
https://sampreetiatta.medium.com/how-
changing-your-thought-patterns-can-transform-
your-perspective-and-boost-your-mood-
75b260f73410

Babich, C. (2020). *Chapter VI: Renaissance and Enlightenment: the golden age of interdisciplinarity.*
Open   Library.
https://ecampusontario.pressbooks.pub/interdi
sciplinarityreformation/chapter/chapter-vi/

Baglieri, S. (2023, January 12). *Understanding why negative thoughts enter the mind and how to push them away.*
LinkedIn.
https://www.linkedin.com/pulse/understandin
g-why-negative-thoughts-enter-mind-how-
salvatore

Balancing act: How to stay informed without getting overwhelmed.
(2024, February 29). LinkedIn.
https://www.linkedin.com/pulse/balancing-
act-how-stay-informed-without-getting-
overwhelmed-nd2ce

Balancing positivity and realism: Recognizing the risks of overly positive thinking. (n.d.). Recovery Direct.

https://www.recoverydirect.co.za/signs-of-unhealthy-positive-thinking/

Bathla, S. (2019, May 20). *6 types of thinking patterns and what should be yours?* Medium. https://medium.com/@sombathla/6-types-of-thinking-patterns-and-what-should-be-yours-acc498492b5a

Beecroft, L. (n.d.). *Learn how to reframe your negative thoughts.* My Well-Being. https://mywellbeing.com/therapy-101/how-to-better-manage-negative-thought-patterns

Being aware of cognitive bias. (2020, February 3). Sergio Caredda. https://sergiocaredda.eu/people/being-aware-of-cognitive-bias/

The benefits of positive language. (n.d.). Intelligent Change. https://www.intelligentchange.com/blogs/read/the-benefits-of-positive-language

BetterHelp Editorial Team. (2024, February 22). *What is mood congruent memory & what can it teach us?* BetterHelp. https://www.betterhelp.com/advice/memory/

what-is-mood-congruent-memory-what-can-it-teach-us/

Blain, T. (2022, August 12). *Feel good foods: The diet-brain connection.* Verywellmind. https://www.verywellmind.com/foods-for-brain-health-5323880

Buddha. (n.d.). Pursuit of Happiness. https://www.pursuit-of-happiness.org/history-of-happiness/buddha/

Buzanko, C. (2024, February 26). *Increasing self-awareness (unleashing resilience part 1).* Dr. Caroline Buzanko. https://drcarolinebuzanko.com/increasing-self-awareness/

Carroll, R. (2021, February 10). *How to thrive when dealing with change.* BetterUp. https://www.betterup.com/blog/adapting-to-change

Carter, S. (2024, April 17). *Perspective, perseverance, and positivity.* CN&CO. https://cnandco.com/2024/04/17/perspective-perseverance-and-positivity/

Celestine, N. (2016, August 30). *Broaden-and-build theory of positive emotions.* Positive Psychology. https://positivepsychology.com/broaden-build-theory/#the-broaden-and-build-theory-of-positive-emotions

Cheong, C. (2022, August 17). *The power of positivity: Why being positive is important for relationship building (with clients).* LinkedIn. https://www.linkedin.com/pulse/power-positivity-why-being-positive-important-clients-clarence

Cherry, K. (2023, January 23). *Effects of lack of sleep on mental health.* Verywellmind. https://www.verywellmind.com/how-sleep-affects-mental-health-4783067

Cherry, K. (2023, February 1). *What is perception?* Verywellmind. https://www.verywellmind.com/perception-and-the-perceptual-process-2795839

Cherry, K. (2023, May 4). *The power of positive thinking.* Verywellmind. https://www.verywellmind.com/what-is-positive-thinking-2794772

Cherry, K. (2023, August 11). *Martin Seligman biography*. Verywellmind. https://www.verywellmind.com/martin-seligman-biography-2795527

Cherry, K. (2024, May 7). *How cognitive biases influence the way you think and act*. Verywellmind. https://www.verywellmind.com/what-is-a-cognitive-bias-2794963

City living and mental well-being. (2021, February 26). American Psychiatric Association. https://www.psychiatry.org/news-room/apa-blogs/city-living-and-mental-well-being

Clear, J. (n.d.). *How to start new habits that actually stick*. James Clear. https://jamesclear.com/three-steps-habit-change

Cognitive distortions—Unhelpful thinking styles (extended). (n.d.). Psychology Tools. https://www.psychologytools.com/resource/cognitive-distortions-unhelpful-thinking-styles-extended/

Cooks-Campbell, A. (2022, October 19). *Adaptability in the workplace: Defining and improving this key skill*.

BetterUp.
https://www.betterup.com/blog/adaptability

Cooks-Campbell, A. (2023, January 23). *How emotions affect learning: The impact of emotions.* BetterUp. https://www.betterup.com/blog/how-emotions-affect-learning

Cooks-Campbell, A. (2023, November 28). *Triggered? Learn what emotional triggers are and how to deal with them.* BetterUp. https://www.betterup.com/blog/triggers

Creating positive spaces. (n.d.). Oliver Health Design. https://globalwellnessinstitute.org/wp-content/uploads/2018/12/biophilicdesignguide-en.pdf

Cunic, A. (2023, February 13). *How to stop negative thoughts.* Verywellmind. https://www.verywellmind.com/how-to-change-negative-thinking-3024843

Cunic, A. (2023, March 3). *What happens to your body when your brain is thinking?* Verywellmind. https://www.verywellmind.com/what-happens-when-you-think-4688619

Cunic, A. (2024, February 12). *7 active listening techniques for better communication.* Verywellmind. https://www.verywellmind.com/what-is-active-listening-3024343

de Almondes, K. M., Agudelo, H. A. M., & Jimenez-Correa, U. (2021, May 20). *Impact of sleep deprivation on emotional regulation and the immune system of healthcare workers as a risk factor for COVID-19: Practical recommendations from a task force of the Latin American Association of Sleep Psychology.* Frontiers. https://www.frontiersin.org/journals/psychology/articles/10.3389/fpsyg.2021.564227/full

Des Marais, S. (2022, September 23). *Cognitive signs of stress.* PsychCentral. https://psychcentral.com/stress/the-impact-of-stress

Developing the mental agility and courage to become self-led. (2023, April 18). Siegfried. https://www.siegfriedgroup.com/understanding-the-role-of-mental-agility-in-individual-leadership/

Dhahan, J. (2023, October 29). *Feedback loops: The art of listening in effective communication.* LinkedIn. https://www.linkedin.com/pulse/feedback-loops-art-listening-effective-communication-jay-dhahan-jmake

Dierking, L. (2016). *Biological consciousness: Stress management through mindfulness and body awareness.* OAC. https://www.obesityaction.org/resources/biological-consciousness-stress-management-through-mindfulness-and-body-awareness/

Duggan, T. (n.d.). *Importance of positive conflict resolution in a team.* CHRON. https://smallbusiness.chron.com/importance-positive-conflict-resolution-team-64182.html

Eating well for mental health. (n.d.). Sutter Health. https://www.sutterhealth.org/health/nutrition/eating-well-for-mental-health

Emotional awareness as a form of communication. (n.d.). University of Cincinnati. https://ucincinnatipress.pressbooks.pub/oralcommunication/chapter/emotional-awareness-as-a-form-of-communication/

Emotional reasoning. (n.d.). Psychology Tools. https://www.psychologytools.com/resource/emotional-reasoning/

Emotional resilience. (n.d.). The Children's Society. https://www.childrenssociety.org.uk/information/young-people/well-being/resources/emotional-resilience

Fidanci, E. A. (2023, June 6). *How architecture can improve mental health?* Illustrarch. https://illustrarch.com/articles/15518-how-architecture-can-improve-mental-health.html

Foynes, M. (2021, May 6). *6 types of family dynamics: from habit to choice.* Holistic Coach. https://melissafoynes.com/types-of-family-dynamics/

Fran. (2022, April 25). *What is a growth mindset and how can you develop one?* Future Learn. https://www.futurelearn.com/info/blog/general/develop-growth-mindset

Gaines, J. (2021, March 23). *How are habits formed? The psychology of habit formation.* Positive Psychology.

https://positivepsychology.com/how-habits-are-formed/

Garey, J. (2023, October 30). *How to change negative thinking patterns.* Child Mind Institute. https://childmind.org/article/how-to-change-negative-thinking-patterns/

Gattig, N. (2023, April 27). *18 effective strategies to improve your communication skills.* BetterUp. https://www.betterup.com/blog/effective-strategies-to-improve-your-communication-skills

George, J. M., & Dane, E. (n.d.). *Mood swing: The hidden role of emotion in decision making.* Rice Business. https://business.rice.edu/wisdom/peer-reviewed-research/hidden-role-emotion-decision-making

Gibson, A. (2023, November 4). *Positive thinking can help mitigate the negative impact of an unhealthy family dynamic during the holidays.* Medium. https://medium.com/authority-magazine/positive-thinking-can-help-mitigate-the-negative-impact-of-an-unhealthy-family-dynamic-during-the-a3327a657c59

Gopinath, P. (2023, September 28). *The power of consistency–How one good habit can transform your life.* LinkedIn. https://www.linkedin.com/pulse/power-consistency-how-one-good-habit-can-transform-your-gopinath

Griffith, A. (2023, September 5). *10 ways to reset your mindset for success.* LinkedIn. https://www.linkedin.com/pulse/10-ways-reset-your-mindset-success-dr-alisha-ali-griffith

Grigg, G. (2024, March 26). *Strategic planning: Visualizing and achieving your business goals.* LinkedIn. https://www.linkedin.com/pulse/strategic-planning-visualizing-achieving-your-business-gordon-grigg-yizdc

Gupta, S. (2024, February 15). *How to tap into a growth mindset and crush your goals.* Verywellmind. https://www.verywellmind.com/growth-mindset-characteristics-benefits-8575613

Habit formation. (n.d.). Psychology Today. https://www.psychologytoday.com/us/basics/habit-formation

Hartney, E. (2023, November 8). *10 Cognitive distortions that can cause negative thinking.* Verywellmind. https://www.verywellmind.com/ten-cognitive-distortions-identified-in-cbt-22412

Hartoonian, N. (n.d.). *The power of visualization: Imagining yourself doing something helps you achieve your goal.* Rowan Center. https://www.rowancenterla.com/the-power-of-visualization-imagining-yourself-doing-something-helps-you-achieve-your-goal/

Harvey, R. (n.d.). *Optimism vs. positivity–What's the difference?* The Resilience Coach. https://www.theresiliencecoach.co.uk/blog/op timism-vs-positivity-whats-the-difference

The Healthline Editorial Team. (2020, March 29). *Causes of stress: Recognizing and managing your stressors.* Healthline. https://www.healthline.com/health/stress-causes

Hempsall, J. (2022, March 16). *Social mobility: Thinking and doing.* LinkedIn. https://www.linkedin.com/pulse/social-mobility-thinking-doing-james-hempsall-obe?trk=public_post

Henley, D. (2022, May 22). *Three strategies to help reframe failure.* Forbes. https://www.forbes.com/sites/dedehenley/2022/05/22/three-strategies-to-help-reframe-failure/?sh=6e2ec4165b48

Herrity, J. (2023, February 28). *How to improve emotional intelligence in 9 steps.* Indeed. https://www.indeed.com/career-advice/career-development/how-to-improve-emotional-intelligence

Heshmat, S. (2020, May 11). *The 8 key elements of resilience.* Psychology Today. https://www.psychologytoday.com/za/blog/science-choice/202005/the-8-key-elements-resilience

History of the power of positive thinking. (n.d.). Self Definition. https://selfdefinition.org/new-thought/articles/positive-thinking-history.htm

Ho, L. (2023, October 10). *The psychology of habit formation (and how to hack it).* Life Hack.

https://www.lifehack.org/889303/habit-formation

Hogan, C. (2021, December 23). *10 ways the media controls your thoughts.* Medium. https://drconorhogan.medium.com/10-ways-the-media-controls-your-thoughts-d2a49434f44d

Hoge, E., & Wulf, C. (2023, September 12). *The case for green space: A cost-effective mental health resource.* ADAA. https://adaa.org/learn-from-us/from-the-experts/blog-posts/consumer-professional/case-green-space-cost-effective

How are physical activity and mental health connected? (2023, October). Mind. https://www.mind.org.uk/information-support/tips-for-everyday-living/physical-activity-exercise-and-mental-health/how-are-physical-activity-and-mental-health-connected/

How can you use visualization to improve your decision-making process? (n.d.). LinkedIn. https://www.linkedin.com/advice/0/how-can-you-use-visualization-improve-your-decision-making-xogef

How can positive conflict resolution improve team performance and morale? (n.d.). LinkedIn. https://www.linkedin.com/advice/1/how-can-positive-conflict-resolution-improve

How does your physical environment affect you and your mental health? (2021, February 24). Newport Institute. https://www.newportinstitute.com/resources/mental-health/physical-environment-affect-you/

How positive thinking can contribute to resilience. (n.d.). Faster Capital. https://fastercapital.com/topics/how-positive-thinking-can-contribute-to-resilience.html

How to benefit from positive thinking. (n.d.). Tony Robbins. https://www.tonyrobbins.com/positive-thinking/

How to build resilience through positive thinking. (2023, October 9). Mediclinic. https://www.mediclinic.co.za/en/infohub-corporate/healthy-life/mental-health/how-to-build-resilience-through-positive-thinking.html

How to improve emotional intelligence. (n.d.). Tony Robbins. https://www.tonyrobbins.com/personal-growth/how-to-improve-emotional-intelligence/

How to improve mental well-being. (n.d.). Mind.org. https://www.mind.org.uk/information-support/tips-for-everyday-living/wellbeing/

How to look after your mental health using exercise. (n.d.). Mental Health Foundation. https://www.mentalhealth.org.uk/explore-mental-health/publications/how-look-after-your-mental-health-using-exercise

Huston, M. (2020, December 27). *What are the characteristics of thriving adults?* Psychology Today. https://www.psychologytoday.com/za/blog/moral-landscapes/202012/what-are-the-characteristics-thriving-adults

Iannarino, A. (2021, April 30). *Why you should filter the content you consume.* Iannarino. https://www.thesalesblog.com/blog/why-you-should-filter-the-content-you-consume

Identifying negative automatic thought patterns. (n.d.). Harvard University. https://sdlab.fas.harvard.edu/cognitive-reappraisal/identifying-negative-automatic-thought-patterns

Indeed Editorial Team. (2023, February 4). *What are cognitive processes? Definition, types, and uses.* Indeed. https://www.indeed.com/career-advice/career-development/cognitive-processes

Itimi, P. (2016, December 31). *How our experience and information influences our perception and understanding of life.* Medium. https://medium.com/@peaceitimi/how-our-experiences-and-information-influences-our-perception-and-understanding-of-life-482fa9af61d8

Jackson, A. (2017, November 20). *Structure your thinking.* LinkedIn. https://www.linkedin.com/pulse/structure-your-thinking-amy-jackson

Jha, N. (2023, June 11). *When the wallet hits the mind:* The connection between economic instability and mental health. Reader's Blog.

https://timesofindia.indiatimes.com/readersblo
g/theeconomicopinion/when-the-wallet-hits-
the-mind-the-connection-between-economic-
instability-and-mental-health-55045/

Journaling techniques for busy people: How to find clarity in five
minutes a day. (2024, March 31). Safe Haven.
https://safehavenbc.com/journaling-
techniques/

Kaltenecker, S. (2015, November 14). *Peer feedback loops:*
how we may benefit and what is needed to realize their
potential. InfoQ.
https://www.infoq.com/articles/peer-
feedback-loops-2/

Kay, N. S. (2017, September 5). *Self-awareness in personal*
transformation. Springer Link.
https://link.springer.com/referenceworkentry/
10.1007/978-3-319-29587-9_22-1

Keen, M. (n.d.). *The importance of a positive mindset in*
modeling. The Models Kit.
https://www.themodelskit.co.uk/blog/the-
importance-of-a-positive-mindset-in-modelling/

Kennedy, K. (2023, April 10). *The ultimate expert-approved diet plan for happier, less-stressed you.* Everyday Health. https://www.everydayhealth.com/wellness/united-states-of-stress/ultimate-diet-guide-stress-management/

Kurland, B. (2020, February 5). *How to shift perspective when you're stuck in your own way.* Psychology Today. https://www.psychologytoday.com/za/blog/the-well-being-toolkit/202002/how-shift-perspective-when-youre-stuck-in-your-own-way

Kurtoğlu, M. B., Yücel, D., Coşkun, E., & Katar. K. S. (2024, April 26). *The relationship between adverse childhood experiences and social anxiety disorder symptoms: The mediating role of rumination.* Springer Link. https://link.springer.com/article/10.1007/s12144-024-06021-5

Lawler, M. (2022, October 22). *Real-life examples of cognitive dissonance.* Everyday Health. https://www.everydayhealth.com/neurology/cognitive-dissonance/real-life-examples-how-we-react/

Leaf, C. (2022, September 26). *The difference between thoughts & memories.* LinkedIn. https://www.linkedin.com/pulse/difference-between-thoughts-memories-dr-caroline-leaf

Lean meat and poultry, fish, eggs, tofu, nuts and seeds and legumes/beans. (n.d.). Eat for Health.gov.au. https://www.eatforhealth.gov.au/food-essentials/five-food-groups/lean-meat-and-poultry-fish-eggs-tofu-nuts-and-seeds-and

Lebow, H. L. (2021, July 2). *How to become aware of negative thoughts.* PsychCentral. https://psychcentral.com/depression/becoming-aware-of-your-depressive-thoughts#keep-a-thought-log

Lewis, R. (2023, October 7). *What actually is a thought? And how is information physical?* Psychology Today. https://www.psychologytoday.com/za/blog/finding-purpose/201902/what-actually-is-a-thought-and-how-is-information-physical

Lijewski, W. T. (n.d.). *Assessing elements of positive psychology.* (n.p.). https://s3.amazonaws.com/EliteCME_WebSite_2013/f/pdf/PYTX05AEI18.pdf

Lindberg, S. (2023, March 23). *How does your environment affect your mental health?* Verywellmind. https://www.verywellmind.com/how-your-environment-affects-your-mental-health-5093687

Loving-kindness meditation: what it is, how to practice and why. (n.d.). Clam. https://www.calm.com/blog/a-loving-kindness-meditation

Luskin, B. J. (2012, March 29). *Brain, behavior, and media.* Psychology Today. https://www.psychologytoday.com/us/blog/the-media-psychology-effect/201203/brain-behavior-and-media

Madeson, M. (2020, July 28). *Logotherapy: Viktor Frankl's theory of meaning.* Positive Psychology. https://positivepsychology.com/viktor-frankl-logotherapy/#frankl

Manage your stress by identifying what triggers it. (2017, November 28). Harvard Business Review. https://hbr.org/tip/2017/11/manage-your-stress-by-identifying-what-triggers-it

Managing your stress in tough economic times. (2023, November 3). American Psychological Association. https://www.apa.org/topics/money/economic -stress

Manstead, A. S. (2018). The psychology of social class: How socioeconomic status impacts thought, feelings, and behaviour. *The British Journal of Social Psychology,* *57*(2), 267-291. https://doi.org/10.1111/bjso.12251

Marteka. (2019, July 15). *12 ways to recognize negative thoughts.* Benevolent Health. https://benevolenthealth.co.uk/12-ways-to-recognise-negative-thoughts/

Mayo Clinic Staff. (2023, November 18). *Stress management.* Mayo Clinic. https://www.mayoclinic.org/healthy-lifestyle/stress-management/basics/stress-relief/hlv-20049495

Mein, H. (2023, September 18). *Designing spaces for well-being through my own experiences.* LinkedIn. https://www.linkedin.com/pulse/designing-spaces-well-being-through-my-own-experiences

Mendel, B. (n.d.). *What is self reflection meditation?* Mindworks. https://mindworks.org/blog/self-reflection-meditation/

Mental health and well-being. (n.d.). Programme of the European Union. https://health.hub.copernicus.eu/mental-health-and-well-being

Miller, K. (2020, March 13). *How to increase self-awareness: 16 activities & tools (+PDF).* Positive Psychology. https://positivepsychology.com/building-self-awareness-activities/#increase

Miles, M. (2022, March 30). *Why learning from failure is your key to success.* BetterUp. https://www.betterup.com/blog/learning-from-failure

Miles, M. (2023, July 27). *10 SMART goal examples for your whole life.* BetterUp. https://www.betterup.com/blog/smart-goals-examples

Mind Tools Content Team. (n.d.-a). *Creative problem solving.* Mind Tools.

https://www.mindtools.com/a2j08rt/creative-problem-solving

Mind Tools Content Team. (n.d.-b). *Emotional Intelligence.* Mind Tools. https://www.mindtools.com/ab4u682/emotional-intelligence

Mind Tools Content Team. (n.d.-c). *Empathy at work.* Mind Tools. https://www.mindtools.com/agz0gft/empathy-at-work

Modern Recovery Editorial Team. (n.d.). *Adapting to change: definition, benefits, and techniques.* Modern Recovery Services. https://modernrecoveryservices.com/wellness/coping/skills/cognitive/adaptability/

Moe, K. (2021, June 4). *5 visualization techniques to help you reach your goals.* BetterUp. https://www.betterup.com/blog/visualization

Moore, C. (2019, January 8). *What is flow in positive psychology? (Incl. 10+ activities).* Positive Psychology.

https://positivepsychology.com/what-is-flow/#positive-psychology-flow

Nash, J. (2015, February 12). *The 5 founding fathers and a history of positive psychology.* Positive Psychology. https://positivepsychology.com/founding-fathers/

Naylor, T. (2016, May 19). *The importance of positive thinking.* LinkedIn. https://www.linkedin.com/pulse/importance-positive-thinking-thomas-naylor

Nicholls, K. (2024, April 11). *Nutrition and mental health.* Nutritionist Resource. https://www.nutritionist-resource.org.uk/articles/nutrition-and-mental-health.html#foodandmoodwhatsthelink

Nutrition and mental health. (n.d.). Beyond Blue. https://beyou.edu.au/fact-sheets/wellbeing/nutrition-and-mental-health

Oppland, M. (2016, December 16). *8 traits of flow according to Mihaly Csikszentmihalyi.* Positive Psychology. https://positivepsychology.com/mihaly-csikszentmihalyi-father-of-flow/

The origins of positive thinking. (2018, January 23). Affirmation Fashion. https://affirmationfashion.com/the-origins-of-positive-thinking/

Outdoor party games for adults. (n.d.). Kombi Keg. https://www.kombikeg.com/blog/party-games-for-adults/

Palmer, m. (2023, November 7). *Types of communication styles and how to identify them.* SNHU. https://www.snhu.edu/about-us/newsroom/liberal-arts/types-of-communication-styles

Patterns of thought. (n.d.). ER Services. https://courses.lumenlearning.com/suny-collegesuccess-lumen1/chapter/patterns-of-thought/

Pennock, S. F. (2024, January 23). *#1 way to break mental health barriers: The thought-action repertoire.* LinkedIn. https://www.linkedin.com/pulse/1-way-break-mental-health-barriers-thought-action-fontane-pennock-dmx4e

Perceptual set. (n.d.). StudySmarter. https://www.studysmarter.co.uk/explanations/psychology/cognition/perceptual-set/

Perkins, L. (2022, March 1). *9 ways to reframe negative thinking into a positive outlook.* Corporate Training. https://corporatetraining.usf.edu/blog/9-ways-to-reframe-negative-thinking-into-a-positive-outlook

Perry, E. (2021a, November 8). *How (and why) to cultivate a positive mental attitude.* BetterUp. https://www.betterup.com/blog/positive-mental-attitude

Perry, E. (2021b, December 3). *Building good habits in your life (and ditching bad ones).* BetterUp. https://www.betterup.com/blog/building-habits

Perry, E. (2022a, March 1). *Get SMART about your goals at work and start seeing results.* BetterUp. https://www.betterup.com/blog/smart-goals

Perry, E. (2022b, May 8). *10 tips to set goals and achieve them.* BetterUp.

https://www.betterup.com/blog/how-to-set-goals-and-achieve-them

Perry, E. (2023a, September 19). *17 positive feedback examples to develop a winning team.* BetterUp. https://www.betterup.com/blog/positive-feedback-examples

Perry, E. (2023b, October 13). *Learn how to stay positive with these 15 tips.* BetterUp. https://www.betterup.com/blog/how-to-stay-positive

Perry, E. (2024a, February 21). *How to change your perspective and change your life.* BetterUp. https://www.betterup.com/blog/how-to-change-your-perspective

Perry, E. (2024b, May 23). *60 positive affirmation examples for resilience and positive mindset.* BetterUp. https://www.betterup.com/blog/positive-affirmations

Pescovitz, D. (2013, October 24). *Secret history of "positive thinking" and the new age.* Boing Boing. https://boingboing.net/2013/10/24/secret-history-of-positive-t.html

Pilat, D., & Krastev, S. (n.d.). *Why do we follow the behavior of others?* The Decision Lab. https://thedecisionlab.com/biases/social-norms

Pollock, D. M. (2023, November 29). *What are cognitive distortions?* Medical News Today. https://www.medicalnewstoday.com/articles/cognitive-distortions

Pomeroy, M. (2021, May 6). *Always be learning: 5 strategies for lifelong learners.* Yoh. https://www.yoh.com/blog/5-strategies-for-lifelong-learners

Reframe Content Team. (2023, December 25). *What are social norms and how do they impact us? Behind the scenes of the social brain.* Reframe. https://www.joinreframeapp.com/blog-post/what-are-social-norms-and-how-do-they-impact-us-behind-the-scenes-of-the-social-brain

Rieck, S. (2021, August 25). *The brain and our habits: Natural pathways to wellness.* Maximus. https://maximus.com/the-brain-our-habits

Robb-Dover, K. (2022, December 7). *Big city or rural: Which is better for mental health.* FHE Health. https://fherehab.com/learning/city-rural-better-mental-health

Robinson, L., Segal, J., & Smith, M. (2024, February 5). *The mental health benefits of exercise.* HelpGuide.org. https://www.helpguide.org/articles/healthy-living/the-mental-health-benefits-of-exercise.htm

Rodriguez, W. (2023, March 1). *The importance of consistency in habit formation: Why small steps lead to big changes.* Medium. https://medium.com/@medzaki55555/the-importance-of-consistency-in-habit-formation-why-small-steps-lead-to-big-changes-fd30a726bb03

Roginski, A. (n.d.). *The long history of the power of positive thinking.* State Library. https://www.sl.nsw.gov.au/stories/long-history-power-positive-thinking

Rubin, G. (2016, February 4). *How to embrace constructive criticism and leave the rest behind.* Next Big Idea Club. https://nextbigideaclub.com/magazine/gretche

n-rubin-embrace-constructive-criticism-leave-rest-behind/5040/

Ryff, C. D. (2022). Positive Psychology: Looking Back and Looking Forward. *Frontiers in Psychology*, *13*. https://doi.org/10.3389/fpsyg.2022.840062

Sandoiu, A. (2017, September 11). *Psychologists find the key to a thriving life.* Medical News Today. https://www.medicalnewstoday.com/articles/319358

Sansom, M. (2022). *10 common thought patterns and how to change them.* Misty Sansom. https://www.mistysansom.com/blog/10-common-thought-patterns-and-how-to-change-them

Santos-Longhurst, A. (2019, February 21). *Benefits of thinking positively, and how to do it.* Healthline. https://www.healthline.com/health/how-to-think-positive

Schaffner, A. K. (2020, September 16). *Perseverance in psychology: Meaning, importance, & books.* Positive Psychology. https://positivepsychology.com/perseverance/

Schiffer, M, E., & William, Y. (2023, November 21). *Selective perception | Definition & examples.* Study.com. https://study.com/academy/lesson/selective-perception-theory-examples.html

Schulcz, P. (2024, January 8). *Adapt and thrive: Lifelong learning as a key to success.* Do Better. https://dobetter.esade.edu/en/adapt-thrive-lifelong-learning-key-success

Scott, E. (2023, October 26). *Why you should keep a stress relief journal.* Verywellmind. https://www.verywellmind.com/the-benefits-of-journaling-for-stress-management-3144611

Segal, J., Smith, M., & Robinson, L. (2024, February 5). *Stress symptoms, signs, and causes.* HelpGuide.org. https://www.helpguide.org/articles/stress/stress-symptoms-signs-and-causes.htm

Self-management—Adopting a growth mindset. (n.d.). Leadership Success. https://www.leadershipsuccess.co/self-management/adopting-a-growth-mindset

Seltzer, L. F. (2017, June 21). *What's "emotional reasoning"– and why is it such a problem?* Psychology Today. https://www.psychologytoday.com/za/blog/ev olution-the-self/201706/what-s-emotional-reasoning-and-why-is-it-such-problem

Shafer, S. (n.d.). *The power of good habits.* Simply Charlotte Mason. https://simplycharlottemason.com/blog/the-power-of-good-habits/

Sheppard, L. (2023, December 25). *Embrace positive thinking for a happier life.* LinkedIn. https://www.linkedin.com/pulse/embrace-positive-thinking-happier-life-lana-sheppard-za9dc

Shero, P. (2019, January 1). *3 Differences between optimism and positive thinking.* Masterminds Leadership. https://mastermindsleadership.com/leadership-blog/3-differences-between-optimism-and-positive-thinking/

Sherwood, A. (2024, March 11). *What is positive thinking?* WebMD. https://www.webmd.com/mental-health/positive-thinking-overview

"Should" *statements.* (n.d.). Psychology Tools. https://www.psychologytools.com/resource/sh ould-statements/

Singh, R., & Petit, C. (2020, February). *Miracle morning routine: 6 steps to transform your life and boost your productivity.* Appvizer. https://www.appvizer.com/magazine/collabor ation/idea-innovation/miracle-morning-routine

Silva, S. (2022, January 11). *15 cognitive distortions to blame for negative thinking.* PsychCentral. https://psychcentral.com/lib/cognitive-distortions-negative-thinking

Sinnett, J. (2022, September 6). *How media consumption impacts your daily train of thought.* University of Calgary. https://ucalgary.ca/news/how-media-consumption-impacts-your-daily-train-thought

Smith, J. (2020, September 25). *Growth mindset vs fixed mindset: how what you think affects what you achieve.* Mindset Heath. https://www.mindsethealth.com/matter/growt h-vs-fixed-mindset

Sparks, Dana. (2019, April 17). *Mayo mindfulness: Know your triggers for stress.* Mayo Clinic. https://newsnetwork.mayoclinic.org/discussion/mayo-mindfulness-know-your-triggers-for-stress/

Stanborough, J. (2023, June 5). *How to change negative thinking with cognitive restructuring.* Healthline. https://www.healthline.com/health/cognitive-restructuring

Star, K. (2023, November 20). *How to overcome all-or-nothing thinking.* Verywellmind. https://www.verywellmind.com/all-or-nothing-thinking-2584173#toc-examples-of-all-or-nothing-thinking

Star, K. (2024, March 20). *How to stop jumping to conclusions.* Verywellmind. https://www.verywellmind.com/jumping-to-conclusions-2584181#toc-examples-of-jumping-to-conclusions

Strawson, L. (2024, January 22). *Embracing positivity and stoicism in everyday life.* LinkedIn. https://www.linkedin.com/pulse/embracing-positivity-stoicism-everyday-life-larry-strawson-pljkf

Stress effects on the body. (2023, March 8). American Psychological Association. https://www.apa.org/topics/stress/body

Stoicism. (2023, January 20). Stanford Encyclopedia of Philosophy. https://plato.stanford.edu/entries/stoicism/

Swaim, E. (2022, July 10). *Emotions can affect your memory—here's why and how to handle it.* Healthline. https://www.healthline.com/health/mental-health/how-does-emotion-impact-memory

Suni, E. (2024, March 26). *Mental health and sleep.* Sleep Foundation. https://www.sleepfoundation.org/mental-health

Sutton, J. (2019, January 3). *What is resilience, and why is it important to bounce back?* Positive Psychology. https://positivepsychology.com/what-is-resilience/

Taylor, M. (n.d.). *Why realistic thinking is better than optimistic thinking.* WebMD. https://www.webmd.com/balance/features/w hy-realistic-thinking-better-optimistic-thinking

Turner, D. (2017, January 5). *Windows of opportunity.* LinkedIn. https://www.linkedin.com/pulse/windows-opportunity-dominic-turner

Understanding social mobility. (n.d.). OECD. https://www.oecd.org/stories/social-mobility/

Understanding the four types of life transition. (2023, July 25). Gemma Brown Coaching. https://www.gemmabrowncoaching.co.uk/post /understanding-life-transition

Vallejo, M. (2023, December 20). *Cognitive distortions for kids: types, examples, and ways to manage.* Mental Health Center Kids. https://mentalhealthcenterkids.com/blogs/arti cles/cognitive-distortions-for-kids

van Son, N. (2023, November 13). *Selective perception: definition, examples, and practical tips.* Tasmanic.

https://www.tasmanic.eu/blog/selective-
perception/

Vilhauer, M. (2023, August 7). *The power of emotions in
decision making.* Psychology Today.
https://www.psychologytoday.com/za/blog/th
e-wisdom-of-anger/202308/the-power-of-
emotions-in-decision-making

Vilhauer, M. (2023, September 11). *Where our negative
thoughts come from.* Psychology Today.
https://www.psychologytoday.com/us/blog/a-
deeper-wellness/202309/where-our-negative-
thoughts-come-from

Villines, Z. (2022, June 20). *Cognitive restructuring and its
techniques.* Medical News Today.
https://www.medicalnewstoday.com/articles/c
ognitive-restructuring

Ward, K., & Stokes, H. (2010, June 21). *Neural plasticity:
4 steps to change your brain & habits.* Authenticity
Associates Coaching & Counseling.
https://www.authenticityassociates.com/neural
-plasticity-4-steps-to-change-your-brain/

WebMD Editorial Contributors. (n.d.). *What is logotherapy?* WebMD. https://www.webmd.com/mental-health/what-is-logotherapy

Webb Wright, K. (2023, March 9). *The power of a mood journal: how writing can help manage emotions.* Day One. https://dayoneapp.com/blog/mood-journal/

Wendt, T. (n.d.). *Hippocampus: what to know.* WebMD. https://www.webmd.com/brain/hippocampus-what-to-know

West, M. (2022, April 21). *What to know about guided imagery.* Medical News Today. https://www.medicalnewstoday.com/articles/guided-imagery#summary

What are reflective practices? (n.d.). University of Minnesota. https://csh.umn.edu/academics/whole-systems-healing/reflective-practices

Whalen-Harris, R. (2023, March 27). *The benefits of positive thinking: Surrounding yourself with positivity.* One Eighty. https://www.one-eighty.org/news/the-importance-of-surrounding-yourself-with-positivity/

Whalley, M. (2019, March 18). *Cognitive distortions: Unhelpful thinking habits.* Psychology Tools. https://www.psychologytools.com/articles/un helpful-thinking-styles-cognitive-distortions-in-cbt/#Cognitive_distortions:_an_introduction_t o_how_CBT_describes_unhelpful_ways_of_thi nking

What is positive perseverance? (2022, June 14). Global Positive News Network. https://www.globalpositivenewsnetwork.com/ what-is-positive-perseverance/

Whitaker, L. (n.d.). *How does thinking positive thoughts affect neuroplasticity?* Meteor Education. https://meteoreducation.com/how-does-thinking-positive-thoughts-affect-neuroplasticity/

Williamson, J. (2019, October 11). *Your environment affects your mindset.* LinkedIn. https://www.linkedin.com/pulse/your-environment-affects-mindset-jody-williamson

Wilson, V. S. (n.d.). *Cultural conditioning: How the world influences our beliefs and behavior.* Exceptional futures. https://www.exceptionalfutures.com/cultural-conditioning/

Wilson, C. R. (2022, May 15). *How to foster positive communication: 9 effective techniques.* Positive Psychology. https://positivepsychology.com/positive-communication/

Winfield, C. (2018, June 21). *Your best self: Build your daily routine by optimizing your mind, body and spirit.* Buffer. https://buffer.com/resources/daily-success-routine/

Wisner, W. (2023, May 12). *Flashbulb memory: What to know about vivid recall.* Verywellmind. https://www.verywellmind.com/flashbulb-memory-7111798

Wisner, W. (2023, January 26). *25 positive daily affirmations to recite for your mental health.* Verywellmind. https://www.verywellmind.com/positive-daily-affirmations-7097067

Woods, T. (2021, November 22). *Why it's important to celebrate small successes.* Psychology Today. https://www.psychologytoday.com/us/blog/1-2-3-adhd/202111/why-its-important-celebrate-small-successes

Young, I. K. (2023, August 15). *Journaling stress relief: 20 daily prompts to manage stress.* DayOne. https://dayoneapp.com/blog/journaling-stress/

Ziozas, G. (2021, August 11). *Thriving: 7 psychological traits to reach your dreams.* Medium. https://medium.com/research-gangster/thriving-7-personal-traits-f4a938f129a7